I0750980

Also by Michael Obiora

Black Shoes

Vivian's Couch

Michael Obiora

On This Day I Thought

On This Day I Thought
by Michael Obiora

Copyright © 2026 Michael Obiora

All rights reserved. No part of this publication may be reproduced, distributed, or transmitted in any form or by any means, including photocopying, recording, or other electronic or mechanical methods, without the prior written permission of the publisher, except in the case of brief quotations used in reviews and other non-commercial uses permitted by copyright law.

First published in 2026 by Open Box Productions LTD

ISBN: 978-0-9930628-2-7

The moral rights of the author have been asserted.

Cover design and interior text and illustrations © Michael Obiora

For those who think and struggle.

On This Day - 6/09/02 - I thought:

There is so much about my past that I wish I could erase,
It's a window of memories
But it's double-glazed.
My mind is so congested
So sometimes it's like a haze.
Negative thoughts – I thought it was just a phase
But it's been happening for months and months, not days.

Feel like I've lost everything – like bankruptcy
Feel like my path has been derailed abruptly.
Places I don't want to be,
Faces I don't want to see... oh Almighty,
Why has this happened to me?

Ideas?
I've come to an end.
Have I really got a true friend?
Were ALL those others really pretend?
No exaggeration to say I could have died,
Don't worry about tears,
Inside I cried.

Spend free time looking for a cheap thrill,
Crosses my mind going back to kill.
Often wonder what it would be like if I befriended a pill.
Want to pick up my things and go AWOL
To pay a visit to my secret friend, alcohol.

Most probably can't think or talk how I talk,
Some might say it but don't walk the walk.
But when you feel high who is there to turn to?
Can anybody tell me what to do?

Turning to things and thinking how I never thought I would.
I ask my reflection: "Am I evil or good?"

All this rotates my mind,
Like an overplaying song
And ends with the question: “was I right or was I wrong?”

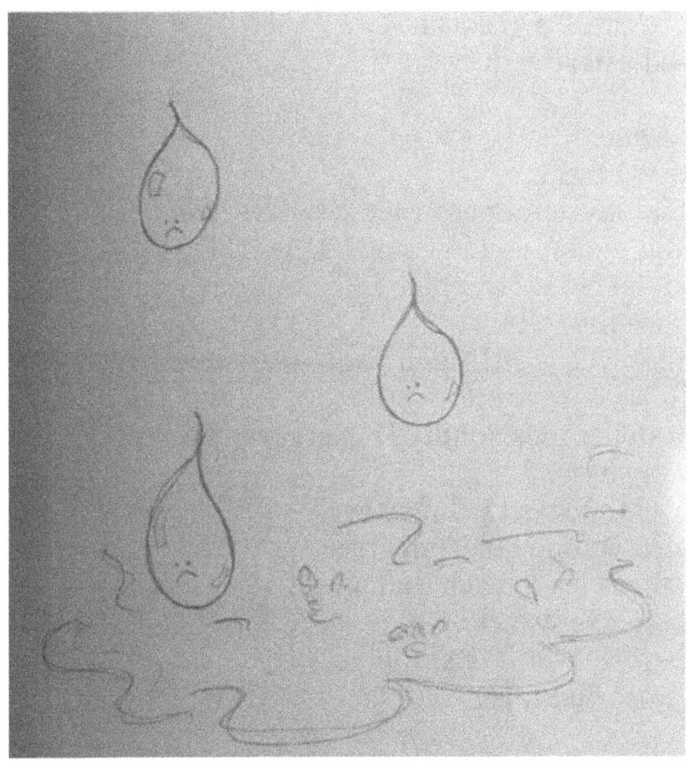

On This Day - 26/11/02 - I thought :

Making moves, taking steps up the ladder,
My acting career is under construction.
Must admit – if not that much but a little bit –
I think about the money it brings,
Women and things.
But that could be the path to self-destruction.
I've got to keep these two down,
So I don't need a head reduction.

Imagine the scene,
And know what I mean
When I say that my great performances have been
Practice for the seduction I'm going to face
When I reach the place I wanna be,
Become the face they all see,
And the brother whose girlfriend females all wanna be.

If there is a watcher then some of it has got to be a test,
But I will try my best
To derail any path to sin they may be
Because I don't want to fall from grace,
Especially before I even reach that place!
And people respect my face.
I want to be a voice people want to hear,
But blowing it is what I fear.

Not yet a foot

But I know where I'm going

So far I've only got one toe in

The door.
I'm gonna knock any obstruction to the floor,
Try not to fuck up anymore.

Because this is all a dream
And not one bit a chore.

On This Day - 24/12/02 - I Thought:

I advise everybody to chase their dream,
The journey may build your self-esteem.
Don't be the person who is looked down upon,
Frowned upon...
Make people think: "He's/She's the one,
Where did you come from?
Can I have some?"

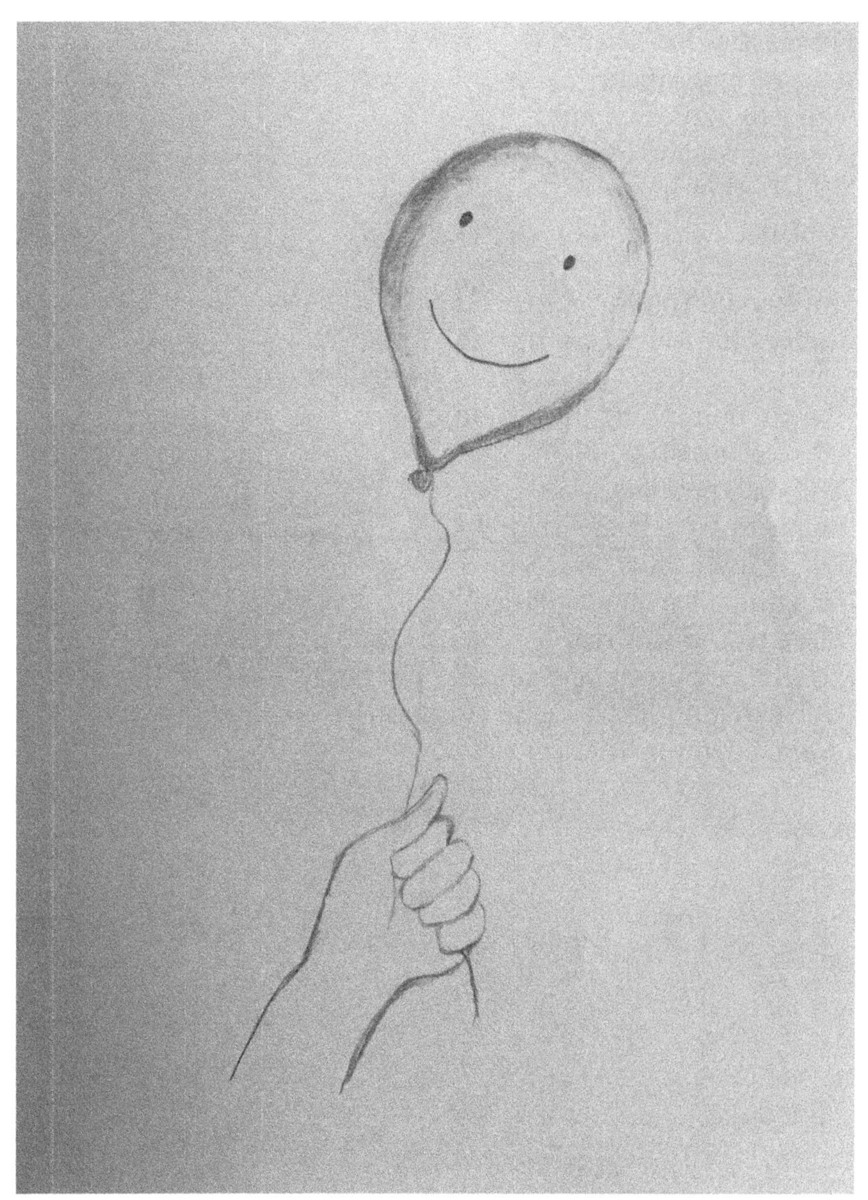

On This Day - 25/12/02 - I Thought:

Whether you're smaller or bigger,
"Wigger" or "Nigger"
Forget it – don't listen to labellers,
It's just ignorance.
"Stick to your own kind" ?
It doesn't make sense!
Act like they know,
But they don't though.
If their thinking were true
How would the world grow?
Their behaviour is see through,

We got something in common;

We're all people.
Lucky to have been created,
Lucky to be alive.
Imagine if we all stuck together,
More would survive.
So let's be honest and not lie,
Oh yeah, another thing in common-
We're all gonna die...

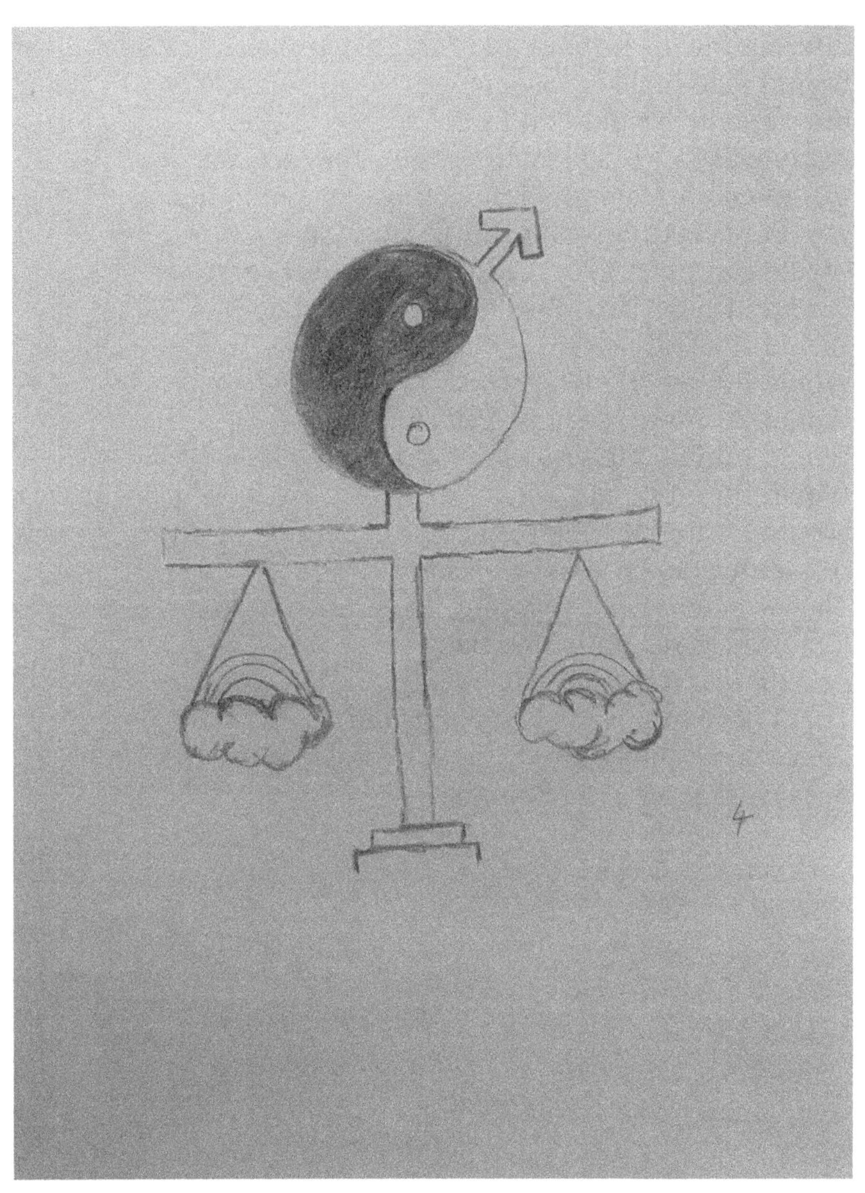

On This Day - I Thought: 26/12/02

I look in the mirror and ask: "do I like myself?"
Yeah, I kind of do
But probably wouldn't if I were someone else.
For one day I would like to see how they see me.
Imagine how scary and interesting that would be.
Would I think "He's arrogant"?
Would the accusations suddenly make sense?
Would I think "He thinks he's better than us"?
Would I be jealous?
Would I think "He looks good"?
Would I want to see him in the nude?
Would I think "He's rude"?
Would I want him to fail?
Would I want his train of success to derail?
It's not nice to be misperceived.
They would only know if they saw how I saw.
I know I am not without a flaw.
And there is no doubt
That I have to sort my bad points out.
That's good, though.
Because it show's I'm human.

So I actually do like myself.

On This Day - 23/10/03 - I Thought:

See the date at the top of this thought,
Take a close look,
It's been a while since I put pen to paper in this book.
Forgive me for being distant
And feeling significantly sad,
My sister, my brother, myself,
Have just lost our dad.
My mother a husband,

"Don't worry, he's in the promised land."

Passing these "beliefs" through each others' brain
Can be the first step to keeping sane.
Unfortunately, honestly, I can't say it eases the pain.
My father, Mr M.C Obiora, was an introvert.
Behind his genius, success, and bad health –
He was ill ridden -
The true extents of his gifts were so cruelly hidden.
When I smile it's a mask of happiness – my mourning hides.
Daddy deserves to be where all good resides.

Me writing this down is my version of thinking aloud.
Everything I do now is to make daddy proud.
Now I am the man of the house,
Feel like mummy, brother and sister are my spouse.
We are so lucky to have had him as a father and in our life.
Our mother was lucky to be his wife.

And heaven is lucky because it has gained an angel.

On This Day - 28/10/03 - I Thought:

When you do it and can say you are busy
You are blessed.
But when you are busy you want rest.
But when you are at rest you are busying your mind
Wondering when you're going to get it next.
So basically if you breathe it,
You're hardly alive.
It would be so much easier to survive on a nine to five.

This is the life of an actor.

On This Day - 17/12/03 - I Thought:

It takes me three hours to get to sleep.
My mind is too busy to count sheep.
When I finally catch them zzzz's
I dream about my dad,
Which is good,
But I wake up and he's not alive,
So then it's bad.
Maybe I don't want to catch the Son of Death for fear of
Being happy when I'm dreaming because I'm seeing my dad,
And waking up and remembering he's not alive
And being sad.
Dreaming is the only time I get to physically "see" him
Or hear his voice.
Should I fall asleep or be tired?
Tough choice.

On This Day - I Thought: 25/12/03

It's Christmas day.
It's been a long time since I believed in Father Christmas.
We're going to be without our father this Christmas.
And for every Christmas to come.
I'm not feeling in a Christmas mood.
There's not even the traditional smell of Christmas food.
But daddy is not here,
So it's no wonder
There's no tree with presents under.

We miss you daddy.

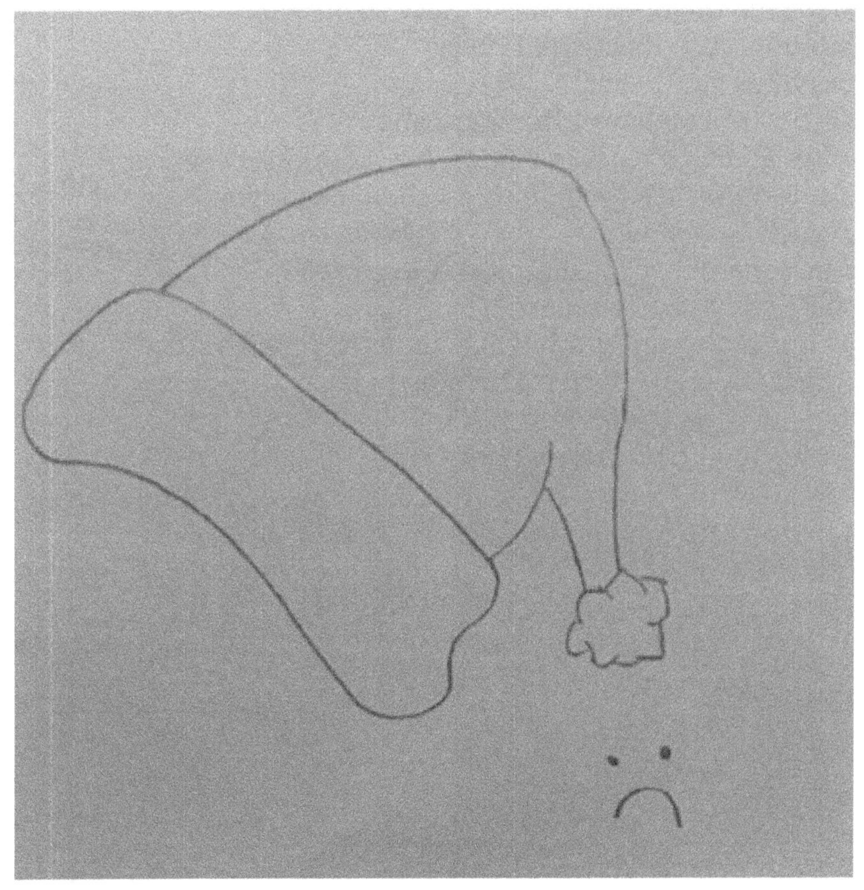

On this Day - 25/12/03 - I Thought:

I've met a girl,
She's stayed in my mind,
That's a start.
But what happens when we grind?
I think she's my girlfriend
But I'm not sure.
She likes me now
But what about when she doesn't anymore?
I kind of hate this sexual energy
Bubbling inside me,
And waiting to erupt like a volcano.
After all these years of being a hoe,
You would have thought that I could just enjoy
A girls' company.
But I guess that's just the weakness in me.
She's sweet, fresh, smart, beautiful.
I hope my complex mind and state she'll understand.
Maybe she can give me a helping hand.
I really hope I don't hurt her.
I am going to be real and not phoney.

Michael?

Remember what you said about ending up lonely?

?
10

On This Day - 31/03/04 - I thought:

I would never like to have a wife like my mother
But I pray my wife can be a mother like my mother.
Introvert? Extrovert?
I don't understand my brother.
My sister from this planet?
Sometimes it's like she's from some weird other.
So when I look in the mirror I feel
Like I'm the only one who's real.
My reflection is not pretend.

I know that I'M MY FRIEND.

:(

On This Day - 5/05/04 - I Thought:

There are three routes of evil in this world:
Money
Racism
Religion
To the second one Doreen Lawrence lost her son.
Eleven years on – case still not solved.
So that evil has won.
People frequently die over the third
Because there are conflicting views of God's word.
There is more than enough of this,
So there should never be hunger or thirst.
I speak about the one written first –
Offer this and the "deaf" suddenly heard.

This is all how the devil preferred.

On This Day - 15/08/04 - I Thought:

Some people say I'm arrogant,

This makes me who I am.
I acknowledge my mistakes,

This proves that I'm a man.

I look in the mirror
And I'm my number one fan.

This path that has chosen me is so insecure.

Slice me in a million pieces,
You'll find determination at my core.

I was planted with this talent
And it's a continuously flourishing seed.

Now you understand my "arrogance"

Because you can see the passion I bleed.

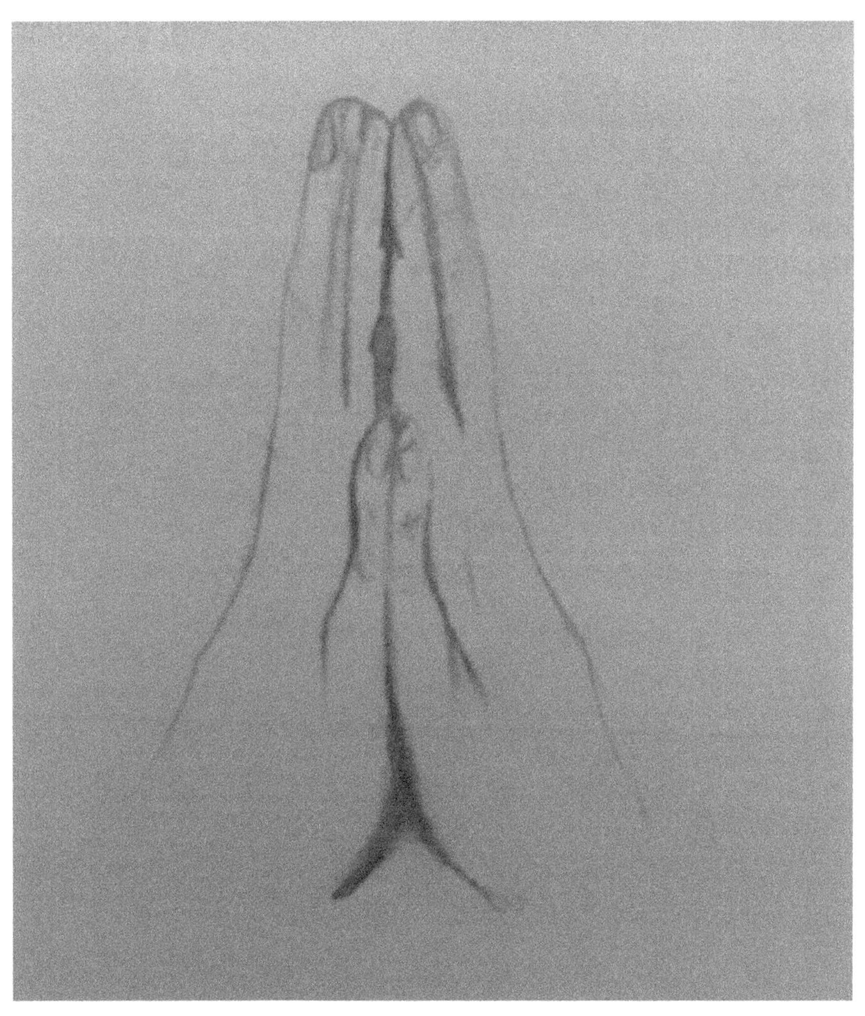

On This Day - 21/12/04 - I Thought:

I woke up today not feeling my best,
I feel fat and need to be told that I'm beautiful.
I look in the mirror at my reflection
And feel rejection
Because there is no answer.
Sudden thought:
I feel very stupid
Because my nineteen year old friend has cancer.
Put things in perspective,
Enjoy life,
Have a positive objective.
Try and make that your answer.

On This Day - 21/12/04 - I Thought:

I don't remember what I did yesterday.
My life has become a whirlwind,
A blur.
I feel isolated,
As if there is no one to whom I can confer.
My mind is incoherent,
I worry about my mother's future
Because she is now a single parent.
What about when we all leave home?
Mummy can't be alone.
I don't know what to do.
Imagine what she's going through.
I'll look after her.
I love you mummy.

On This Day - 21/12/04 - I Thought:

My career is the best that it has ever been,

But my happiness remains to be seen.
Deeper and deeper the internal pain is embedding.
Illustrated,
Annunciated,
And reiterated by the fact that my father won't be at my Wedding.

I have the most beautiful girlfriend whom I have been so vulnerable with,

Maybe too honest and let my meaningful emotions unfold.
She soaked all this up,
Yet I treated her so cold.

You can see I shy away from consistently conveying my feelings on this paper

Because I feel that compared to the last
It has to be written greater.

Fuck that.

If on a scale of one to ten you give this nought,

I can't deny that at this time,

Here is what I thought.

:/

On This Day - 21/12/04 - I Thought:

Wondering if there is someone for me on this earth.
Want my love to be as if she gave me birth.
My significant other
Must be like my mother.
I need to be looked after,
Thrown in the air and caught amidst fits of laughter.
Tucked into bed and given medicine when I'm feeling sickly.
This is all because I grew up too quickly.

On This Day - 21/12/04 - I Thought:

In love with love
And a fiend for friendship.
This sentence is synonymous with me.
I long for a soul mate,
The idea of the purest kind of care thrills me.
Every time I think of being without these things

It kills me.

I can’t be alone.

:(

On This Day - 26/08/05 - I Thought:

When we crossed the road

You used to hold my hand

Now confiding is rare

This I don't understand

I took pleasure in tying your shoelace

Currently we live together
But it's like we're each in a different place.

Your voice has decreased in tone

You never answer your phone

You are a self inflicted stranger.

I wonder if this can be salvaged

Because we lived harmoniously

Then you grew up unceremoniously.

Apparently, the only stronger love is that of a child and Mother

If this is the case what happened to my little brother?

:(

On This Day - 27/04/06 - I Thought:

I think he's really attractive,
Gorgeous in fact.
His skin is dark chocolate,
And I really like that.
He has achieved so much at such a young age,
This is an aphrodisiac.
I'm coming out the closet,
They'll support me in this and not react with horror,
Because I am talking to the mirror.
I proudly acknowledged and sought professional help,
Enabling me to fall back in love with myself.

<3

On This Day - 27/04/06 - I Thought:

I'm combating it but there's something anchoring me.
At times I feel it in my stomach
But it's not something I ate.
It's harder to expatiate.
It's also external,
Attached to my skin.
It accompanies me everywhere,
Like a Siamese twin.
This green thing took up residence in my torso
And it must be ejected.
I want to applaud for someone else
And say: "envy I rejected."

36

On This Day - 11/09/06 - I Thought:

I thought I was number one,
Maybe in this thought I was on my own
And it feels as if I have been knocked off my throne

I learned how to throw up my fist
But apparently at the party I won't be missed

I've been in this womb for twelve years,

Working consistently for worth.
Surely this past year has been time for my birth?

Experiences so fast,
It bewilders me that I have suddenly been surpassed.

The advice that I've been given
Is that my time will come.
I am now deaf to this because

I thought I was number one

...............O

On This Day - 4/05/07 - I Thought:

If my family are my world
Then I am tired of carrying the weight of the
World on my shoulders.
I am tired of dragging along boulders.
I am not even the oldest,
But I'm certainly the boldest.
If this pressure continues
I will end up the coldest.
Nobody to advise me,
Nowhere to run.
The day I lost my father
I also lost my mum.
Suddenly no parents, so to my remaining parent
I assumed that role.
So, prematurely I became an old soul.

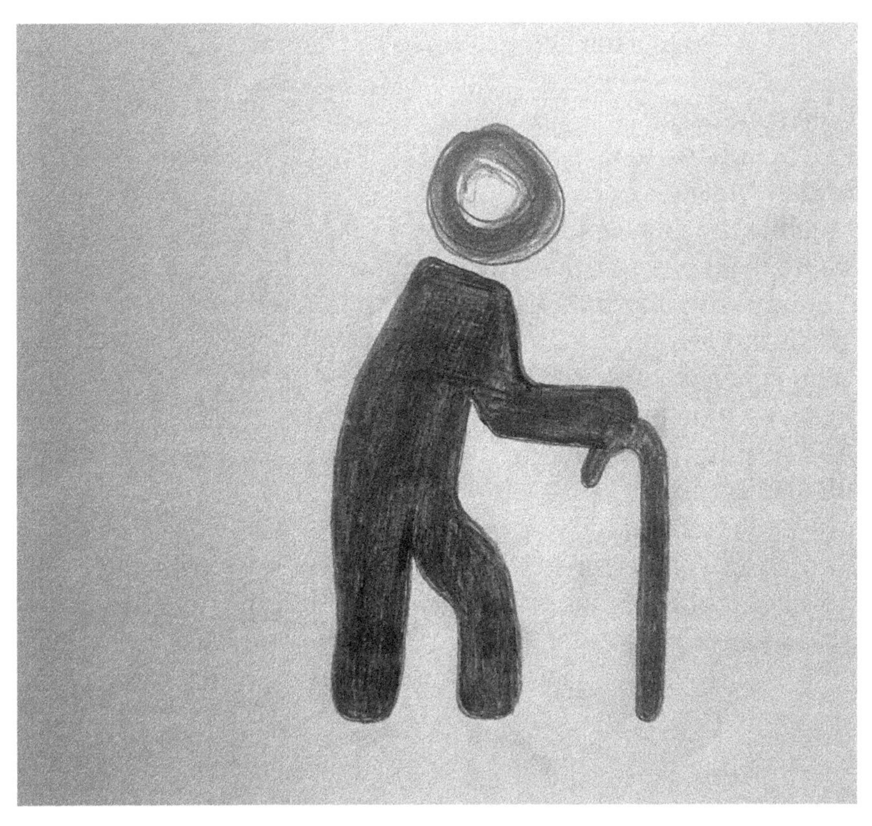

On This Day - 4/05/07 - I Thought:

I am so lonely.
I have nobody to ask.
And even when I do,
I dislike the answers I receive.
There is no one to drive me to achieve.
Nobody with anything exciting up their sleeve.
Why am I always the life and soul of the party?
Who is here to entertain me?
I give so much out,
And nothing comes in.
I feel empty.
My soul is vacant.
This charisma of mine has been at my energy's expense.
So leaving this planet is the only thing that makes sense.

On This Day - 4/05/07 - I Thought:

When my emotions are gathering momentum
I try to be unbiased and attempt to stop...
At which point,
Deciding to weigh things up;
One hell of an adventure,
A montage of fun.
Flashbacks of adversities
That I am proud to have overcome.
But parallel lies the loneliness that I can't outrun.
Futile trying to work it out.
It's nonsensical from any which angle,
Especially when you consider
That I am not even single.

:/

On This Day - 26/09/07 - I Thought:

One of my truths that I have come to comprehend
Is that my outgoing love has an end.
At sixteen its' distribution was brought out ferociously.
So now I guard it jealously.
The love I give must now be equal to an unmoving see-saw.
If you have all your family,
What do you need me for?

On This Day - 26/09/07 - I Thought:

Afro-centricity is a part of my personality.
It is something that will never cease to be.
But I wonder if it has held me back.
Some of my actions have garnered smiles to my face.
But it seems as if few of my own have the same ideas
In the first place.
I look around and I am younger than most.
When it's time to act they turn into ghosts.
They are controlled by fear.
But I speak loud and clear
And will never whisper.
Again they will smile when I initiate prosper.
I'm not in anyway looking for a friend
But it's about time I looked around and saw men.

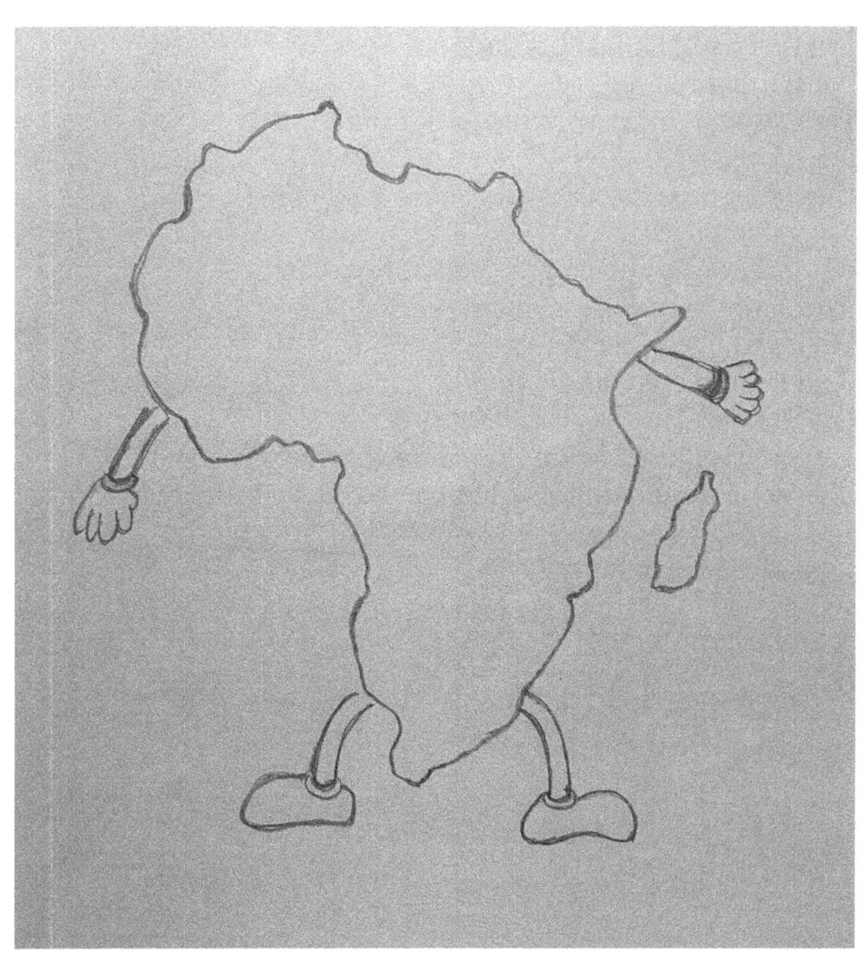

On This Day - 5/04/08 - I Thought:

A thirty-year old cried to me
That he had just lost his dad.
No sympathy I felt
He had more time with his father than I had.

The bitterness that loss can cause made me feel sad.

My father was alive for sixteen of my years,
Thirty of the mans',
He loved his father
And I completely understand.

Imagine if I had known my father for thirty years,
One could argue that it could have cost twice the tears.

On This Day - 13/03/10 - I Thought:

I feel I only exist in my head,
So I'm afraid to open my eyes.
Most people look to the skies,
Wondering where they go when one dies.
Me?
I'm more concerned with where my future lies.

Not sure if I'm from here
Or temporarily visiting this planet.
They say 'The world is yours,'
But can an alien have it?

If I'm not a human being,
Against what do I measure my worth?
To what rules do I abide if
Earth was not the place of my birth?

Is when I open my eyes the dream,
And shut them the real?
Am I superhuman-
The man of steel?

I zone out in a room full of people
And that cannot be right.
Is this the wrong world for me?
Is this my kryptonite?

That's why I seek solace in the alternate
Life in my head.
Because when I open my eyes
I might as well be dead.

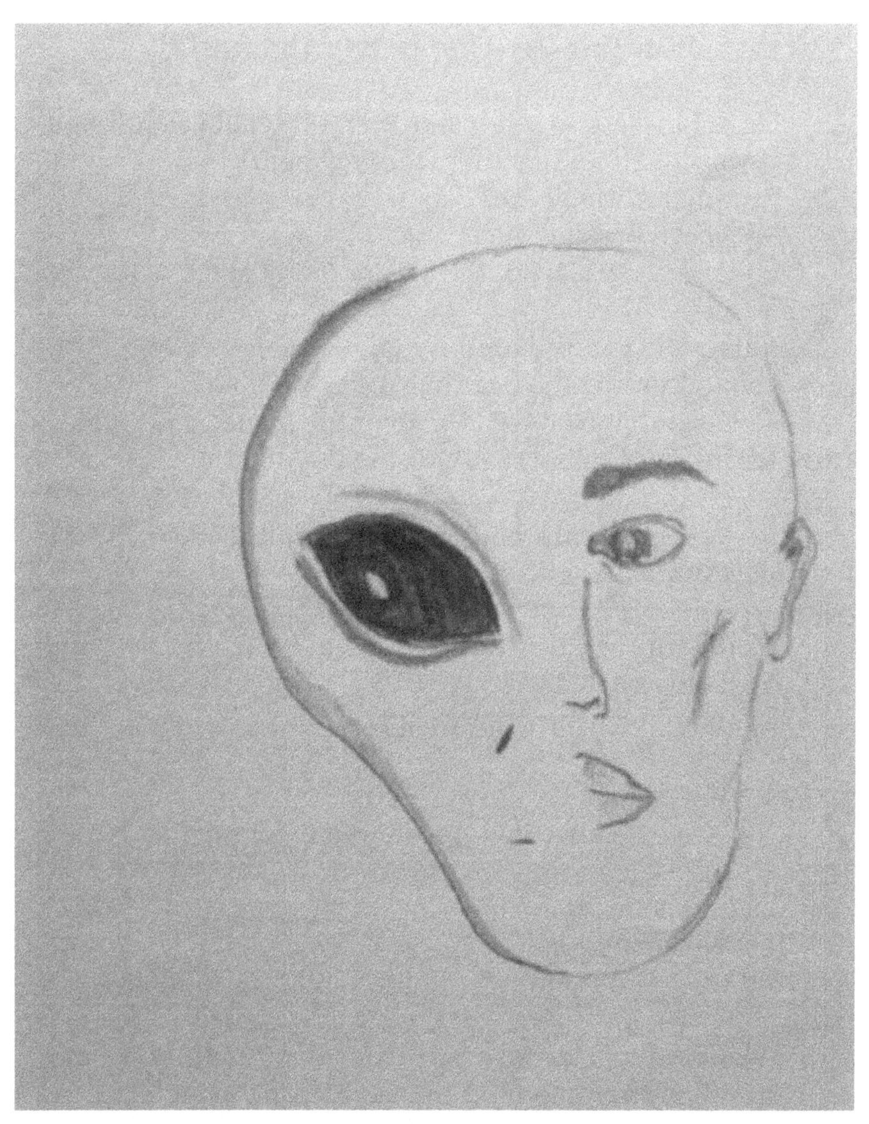

On This Day - 3/04/10 - I Thought:

Have I locked myself inside an impregnable vault?
Is this loneliness I suffer from my fault?
Running through life,
My youth passing me by.
My only view is from the corner of my eye.

Constantly focused on the goal,
Not addressing the fact that there is a hole.
Haven't stopped once to take in the scene
Because all I'm doing is chasing the dream.

Never considering what's in my periphery,
Ignoring those who clearly love me.

Racing through the tunnel
With only one vision.
Relentlessly jostling for pole position.

Getting a job is my only pit–stop.,
Don't tell me anything 'cos I already forgot.

Success is my fuel.
It's what drives me.
But this road is empty if I haven't got my family.

I want to fly to the sky until there is nothing above me,
But I have to remember the people who love me.

The time has come to give out the code to my vault,
Or this lonely life I lead will remain my fault.

On This Day - 01/05/10 - I Thought:

When I think of her
I am overcome with guilt.
I've left her uncovered,
Like she's sleeping with no quilt.
I'm so sorry mother
For not providing you cover.
But above,
The burden I felt from you
Continues to hover.
You talk but I don't listen.
My mind is some place other.

Your love is so close
But I've pushed you away.
Thank you for never giving up on me.
Tomorrow's a new day.

On This Day - 08/08/10 - I Thought:

Who is this 'They" that is always referred to?
"They" is the most famous person in the world.
But what does this so-called "They" look like?
Is "They" a boy or a girl?

"They" say I won't make it.
"They" say I can't take it.
Is "They" dark?
Is "They" light?
You know what "They" say..?
"Two wrongs don't make a right."

But I've got to keep going.
I've got to keep growing. Despite what "They" may say.
After all,
How could I ever let a faceless group called
"They'"get in my way?

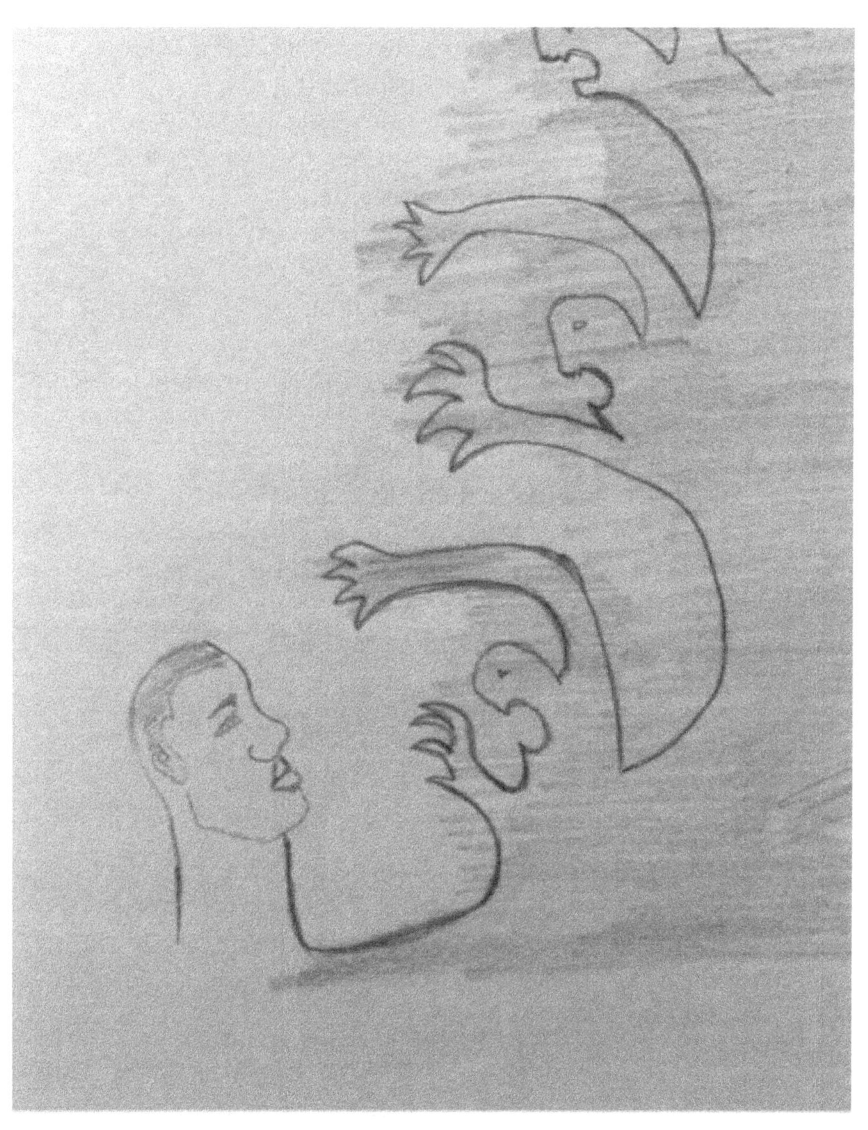

On This Day - 20/11/11 - I Thought:

I only exist between “action” and “cut.”
So when the cameras stop rolling
Everything stops.
It’s like talking on the phone
And the line suddenly goes dead.
So I have to revert to existing in my head.

I’ve lost interest in the small talk
And complaints of my peers.
I’m so sick and tired of hearing about their fears.
Misery loves company
But they won’t find it in me...
The director just called “action,
So I’m now set free
To be who the story needs me to be.

The character is when I’m awake.
My life is when I’m sleeping.
This rest will not be stirred by any ungrateful
Weeping.

I get home and the low is about to come.
So I think of the next chapter,
To keep the momentum.
Because I’ve been repeatedly let down by my team,
I’m forced to exist in my head
And continue to dream.

On This Day - 17/12/11 - I Thought:

I can't lose my cool with a fool
Because an onlooker can't tell who is who.
I can't lose my cool with a fool
Because then it would matter that
I was kicked out of school.

I can't jeopardise
How high I can rise
For those worthless traps in disguise.
No matter how much they dare,
Myself they won't snare.
Because as soon as I'm shackled
Society won't care.

Since I know this too well,
On it I won't dwell.
I'll never let it be said;
"Famous actor fell."

Being a mere mortal,
It's easier said than done.
But each pitfall avoided
Is a battle I've won.

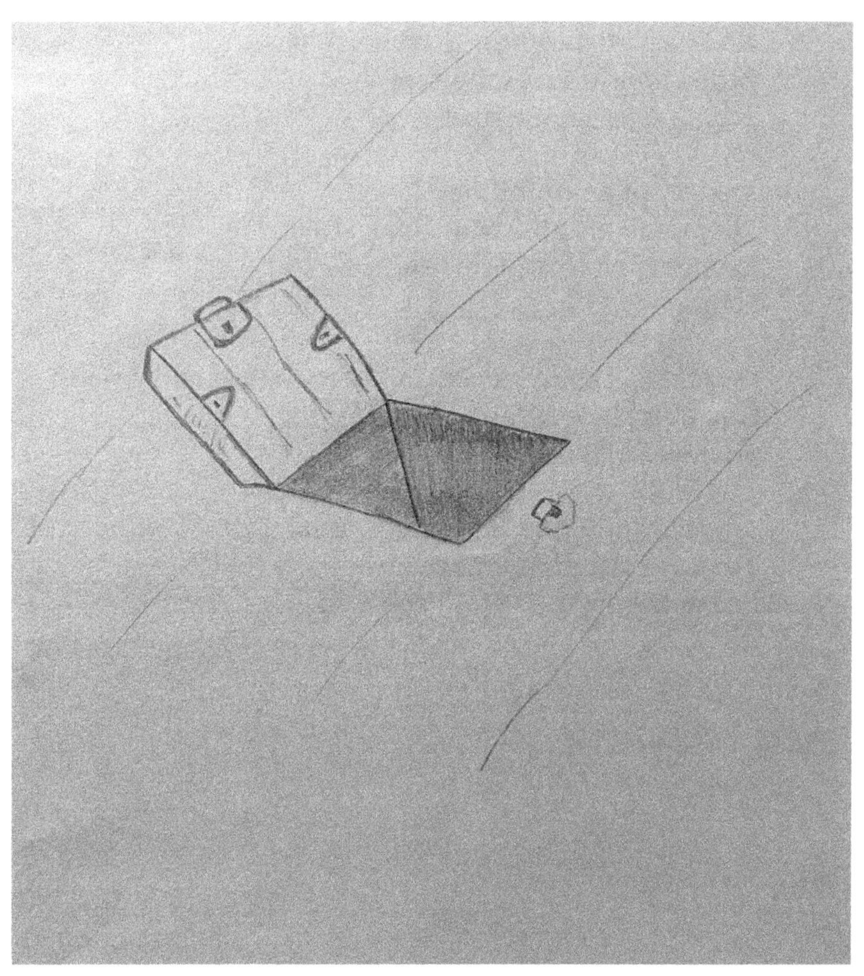

On This Day - 15/03/12 - I Thought:

Jealous of living icons
So I seek inspiration from those past.
Since they are no longer here
I can't fear coming last.

Anxiety of an unfulfilled fate
Threatens my ability to congratulate.
Recognising this in myself
Is an image I hate.

I want it so badly; a cocktail of ambition and greed.
One must lack balance
To have such a selfish need.

This is why I pray that I'm blessed
To have something more important than me –
Because only then will I cease to live so selfishly.

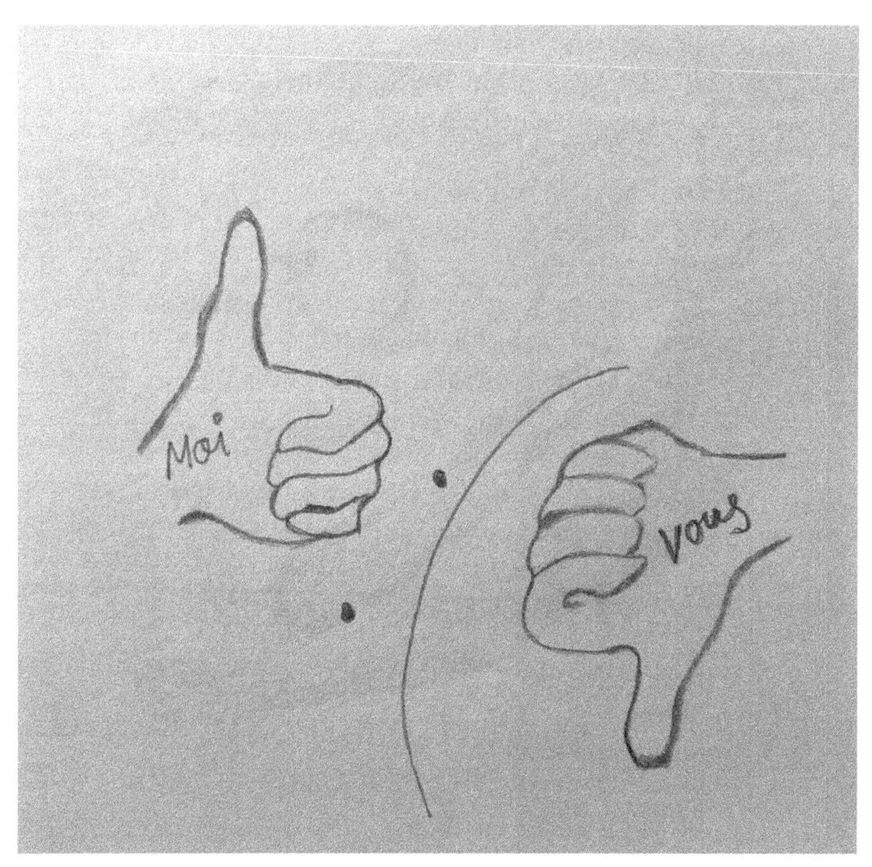
Moi
Vous

On This Day - 5/09/12 - I Thought:

For me sleep on them is rare.
I find it hard to drift away whilst upright in the air.
I wish to sample all the world,
So it's unavoidable.
But to be the only one awake
Amongst strangers is unenjoyable.

The pretty staff affix their well rehearsed smiles
At every sign of turbulence.
The trolly's are rattling and the ocean is below,
So their calmness is of no relevance.

Exchanging emotionless looks with fellow passengers -
We're clearly ignoring the elephant.
As we rattle along from side to side,
I pray for luck heaven sent.

I like taking the one that eases my pains,
I love flying
But I hate planes.

On This Day - 14/10/12 - I Thought:

She told me that I'm crazy.
This I could not deny.
The voice in my head
Dared me to reply.
I ignored the challenge and knew she would cry
Because I saw a tear form in the corner of her left eye.

One minute we're so happy,
The next we're the opposite.
When I'm aching she'd rather take the brunt of it.

I know there is only so long she can carry this burden,
Her heart is so soft
But it's beginning to harden.

She asked me why our love is a tightrope,
And then she confessed she's beginning to lose hope.
I promise her I'm strong - I'll be back,
It won't unfurl.
How sad it is to have your sanity
Questioned by your own girl.

On This Day - 13/06/13 - I Thought:

I'm morphing into a closed book
And I'm running out of people I'll allow to take a look.
Call it paranoia.
Call it mistrust.
But how can I find a real friend if I do not open up?

My increasingly guarded state
Is symptomatic of my scars,
Instead of talking to someone
I'd rather inhale and go to mars.

Spending so much time alone
I can hear my heart beat.
I promise myself It'll all change
When I'm back on my feet.
Therefore I spend my existence
Treating everything as temporary.
But I know that if I continue to alienate
There will never be a friend for me.

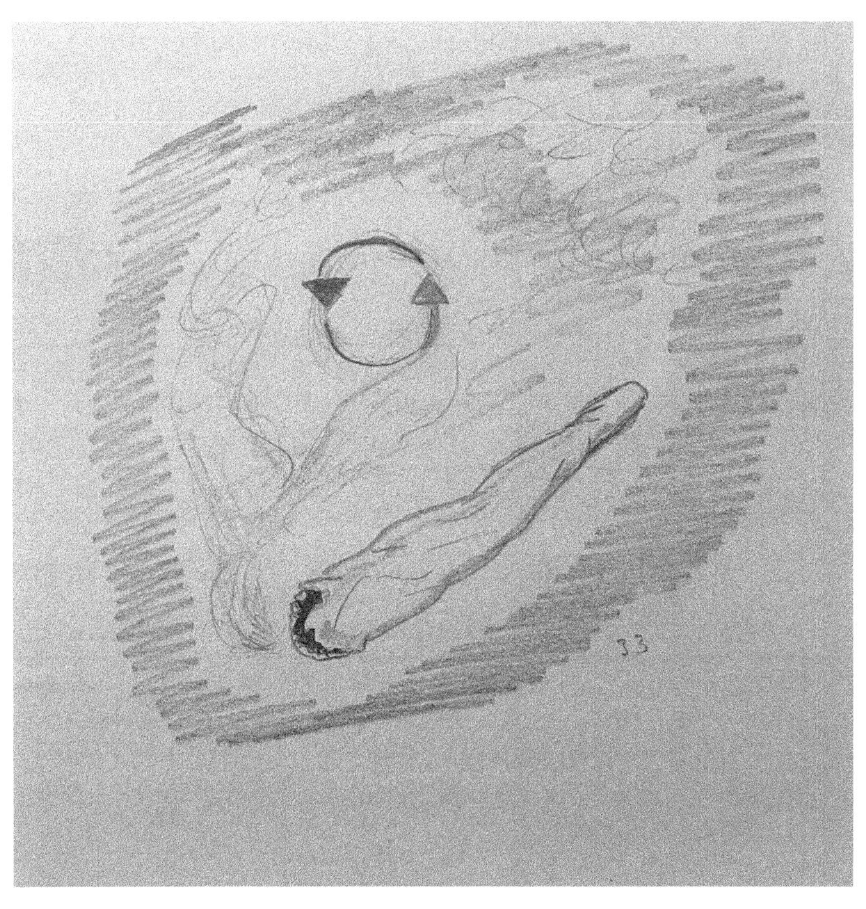

On This Day - 13/06/13 I Thought:

I have no family,
Oh woe is me.
When she tells me about hers
I suppress my jealousy.
My bitterness is turning me into what

I've been running from my whole life.

How can I be envious of my future wife?
If it was infidelity it would make sense.
If it was just my insecurities
I may have a defence.

But seeing the house of love she used to share
Highlights the fact that my past remains

In a state of disrepair.

I tell myself that she can teach me the values I desire
But if I told you I wasn't scared of falling short,
I'd be a liar.

On This Day - 1/07/13 - I Thought:

As far back as I can remember
I've never been in the room.
Whatever it was that I was doing,
I'd be thinking about what I'd be doing soon.
I really wish for one moment
That I could actually live for the moment.
I don't know when I will cease to believe
That the grass is greener,
I sadly apply this to my relationship
And not only my career.
This is wholly unjustified since my woman's
Love and kindness towards me is so sincere.
I'm disliking my reflection more and more
And my conscience remains unclear.
Being unable to put this behind me,
And be grateful and content
Is becoming my biggest fear.

On This Day - 12/07/13 - I Thought:

The rare sun shines bright outside,
But I'm annoyed because I have no plans
And I'm inside.
My phone has been quiet
And I feel empty inside.
Now it rings - it's family, not work
So I toss it aside.

Now the sun is setting
And the temperature drops,
I can breathe a sigh of relief
Because the sadness temporarily stops.

Although I love the heat,
And that will always remain true,
I like it best when I'm working
Otherwise I have nothing to do.

On This Day - 24/07/13 - I Thought:

I can pass it off as honour,
And I can simply call it standards,
But why is it every other day my lips curl downwards?
Perhaps I would more often smile
If my lack of forgiveness went on hiatus for a while.
Maybe if I opted to stop being true to myself
To the end
I wouldn't have to keep searching for a friend.
Could it possibly be
That I could naturally sleep at night
If my personality wasn't so Black and White?

I'm thinking depression
Could be my former condition,
If it were in my nature to temper my ambition.

Sat in solitude I ponder the thought
That if I wasn't so irritable
My company would be more desirable.

Then I look in the mirror
And things albeit temporarily become clearer
Because that face and soul belongs to me.
And though I am definitely open to change,
Right now I don't know how else to be.

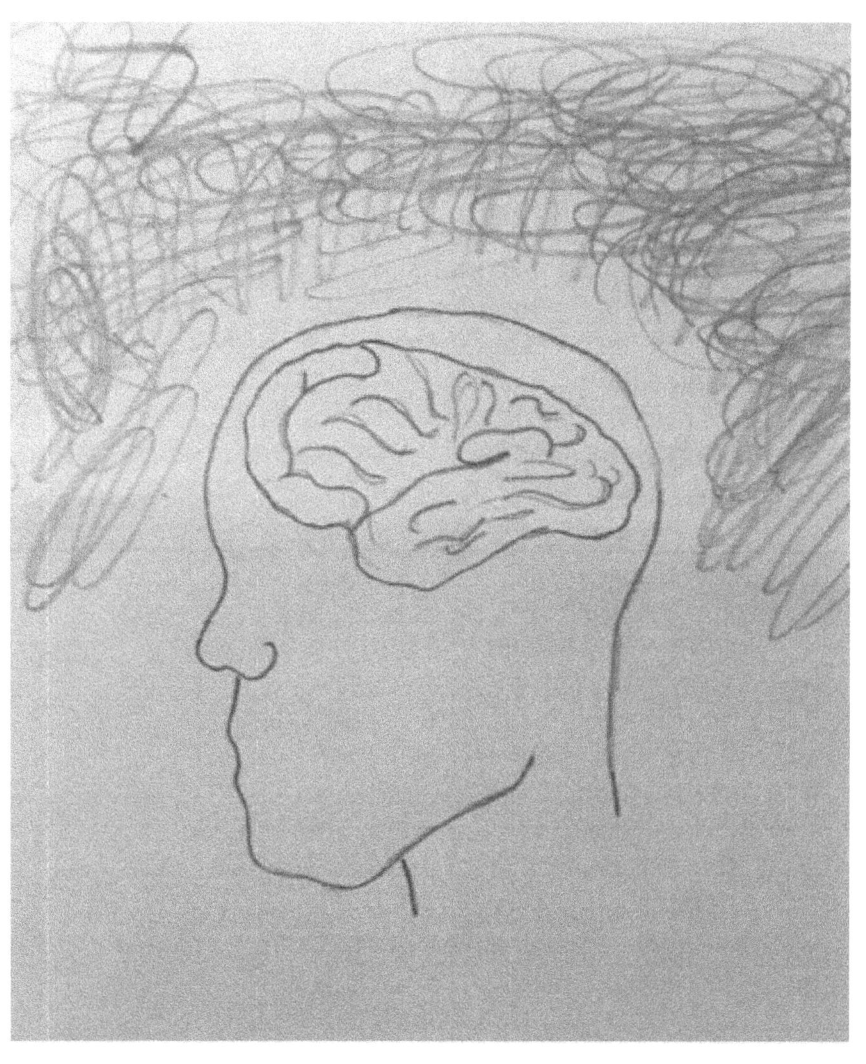

On This Day - 23/08/13 - I Thought:

F ickle,
A ll of a sudden no interest when you're not working.
M ost people crave it.
E verybody look how great my life is on Facebook!

On screen and get recognised
Everybody wants a photo.
Raising money for charity?
Buy my book? - that's a no no.
A new follower on twitter -
Lot's of fans:
"We love you M.O"
Off-screen,
Unemployed,
Now you're riding solo.

It's easy to congratulate "a star"
When they're in the sky,
But do you know how to comfort them
When work is passing them by?
I refuse to feel sorry myself
Because life can be so much more unfair.
"Shit happens."
Oh believe me I've had my fair share.
But about the fickleness of celebrity
I'm fully aware.
And please don't ever think
That I'm convinced you truly care.

37

On This Day - 23/08/13 - I Thought:

I wish I truly believed in God
Because it would make my life more bearable.
But I cannot find it within myself
To have faith in the intangible.

I've known those who worship weekly
Bark, bite, and challenge non-belief,
Then when tragedy has hit
Some of these people suddenly have no teeth.

I'm familiar with people
Who have sat in one place and have said,
"Whatever will be, will be."
But I've only known hard work
So I'm not sure that mentality would set me free.

"He's gone to heaven," I said
As they laid the wreath.
"There is no heaven!" She sobbed,
Even though she wore a crucifix underneath.

Faith can guide one,
So nobody needs to explain their "how" and/or "why."
But I could never feign religion
Because that would be an uncomfortable lie.

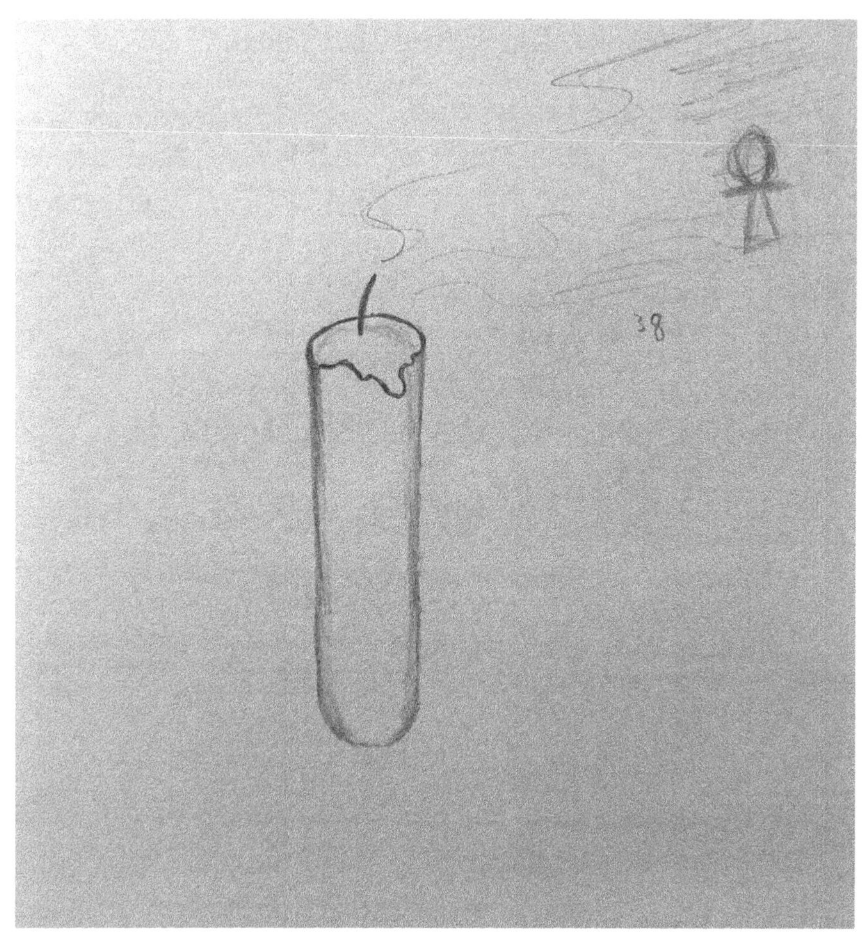
38

On This Day - 23/08/13 I Thought:

A sea of faces as I look back -
I've met some characters along the way.
The couple that upgraded my flight for me -

I'll never forget that day.
But suspicion
And lack of trust led me to keep them at bay.

What kind of life is it
When you wonder why somebody is talking to you?

Symptomatic of attention from a young age,
And working since nine years old
Earning a good wage.

"Don't mention to my friends that you're down

And not working."

This was said by the woman that birthed me.
She's incredibly kind,
So I do not believe she intended to hurt me.

But now as far as I'm concerned
Her true colours she'll never be able to conceal

Perhaps if this wasn't the mentality of the person

Who attempted to raise me

I would have seen some of the amazing people

I've met as real.

On This Day - 22/09/13 - I Thought:

After all those years on the stage,
I started to feel jaded at twenty two years of age.
Now I'm twenty six and it feels even worse,
Could it be that starting work at nine
Has turned out to be a curse?
It's a fight to keep the hunger,
And a battle to remain enthused.
But my less experienced peers are hungry
So I've got too much to lose.

Imagine being put on a pedestal
By your friends, classmates and mother.
Try to envision the jealousy that this can bring about
From your own sister or brother.
If such has been your existence
For almost a third of your life,
To not get praised or recognised
Is likely to cut like a knife.

I have to admit that if I could go back
I would possibly seek an alternative.
Because to be constantly chasing,
Exhausted and paranoid,
Is not a way to live.

:/

On This Day - 29/10/13 - I Thought:

I've decided that there is more to life than acting,
There are far more important things in the world.
But do I really believe this?
Or is it because my tightly wrapped plans
Have unfurled?
I am young and ambitious,
So shouldn't my career be my world?

I am selfish and have no children,
What else am I supposed to want?
But I am not feeling well,
It would be unhealthy to front.

Every time I see my reflection
I wonder who I am supposed to be.
I got kicked out of school at fifteen -
Either way I didn't have a plan B.
I was a soldier back then,
But will it eventually be the undoing of me?
The last twelve years have been extremely costly
And I'm paying with my sanity.

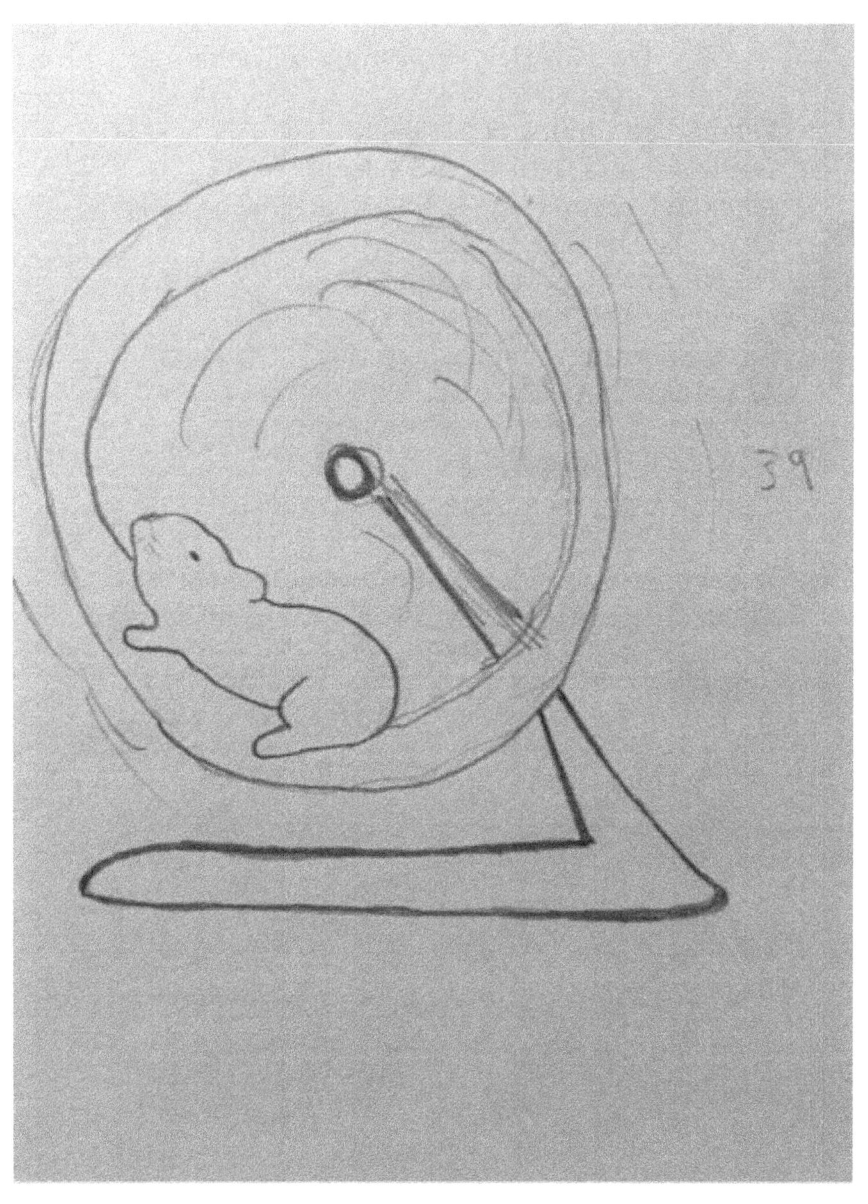
39

On This Day - 29/10/13 - I Thought:

I should be smiling at her beauty
While she lays there sound asleep.
I should be remarking at how peaceful she looks
Enveloped by our sheets.
I should wrap my arms around her
And make her feel safe while she dreams.
But I am jealous that she's resting -
As pathetic as that seems.

It says a lot about myself
That I even contemplated blaming her.

It has to be up there with my lowest moments
That I've made her feel guilty about my insomnia.

41

On This Day - 5/12/13 - I Thought:

One should never put all their eggs in one basket at all,
But it absolutely crushes me when I don't get that call.
The fact that this is all I do
Reminds me that I have nothing to catch me
Whenever I stumble and fall.

I keep my phone attached to me
Every single day,
If it rings other than for an opportunity
Then it gets in the way.
I constantly ask myself if I have become mean
Because I'd rather see 'Agent'
Than anybody else on my screen.

I am so fucking angry,
I am so fucking down.
Unemployment provides too much time
And the thoughts bounce round and round.

She told me I'm a pessimist,
But how can that be,
When I achieved so much
In a career that is built upon fantasy?
I must push that conversation aside
And tell myself not to be sulky
Because quite simply
She'll never know what it's like to be me.

Despite all the battles,
The scars and the weariness,
Somehow, some way,
I'm able to see through the mess.

I wake up everyday with a feeling of optimism,
And try to approach all with pragmatism

It's so damn hard,

But I'm harder on me.

So it's time I applauded myself
For maintaining some discipline.
I must acknowledge the good,
Instead of only subjecting myself to criticism.
I am doing my best,
And I am ready for every chance,
I have to believe that I will supersede my circumstance.

On This Day I - 29/01/14 - I Thought:

It's a new year,
And time for a fresh start.
"The next twelve months are going to be great."
Did this come from the heart?
Did I really believe this?
Or was it just to keep me sane?
I can't really answer that,
To me it's not simple and plain.
But the fact of the matter is that
I'm about to get on a plane.

I finally received the call
That reversed my fall.
And in a single bound
I could see over the wall.

I resent the fact that something
Has such a hold on me,
But a successful actor is all I've ever wanted to be.
Now I'm caught between celebration
And fear of the lack of control
I have over my vocation.
In my next breath I'm experiencing
The pride of my motivation.

I remained ready for this opportunity,
And that is no mean feat
Because for ten months I woke up unemployed
And that felt like defeat.
But the storm is over
And it'd be wrong not to acknowledge this triumph
Because who knows what would have happened if
I was out of work for another month?

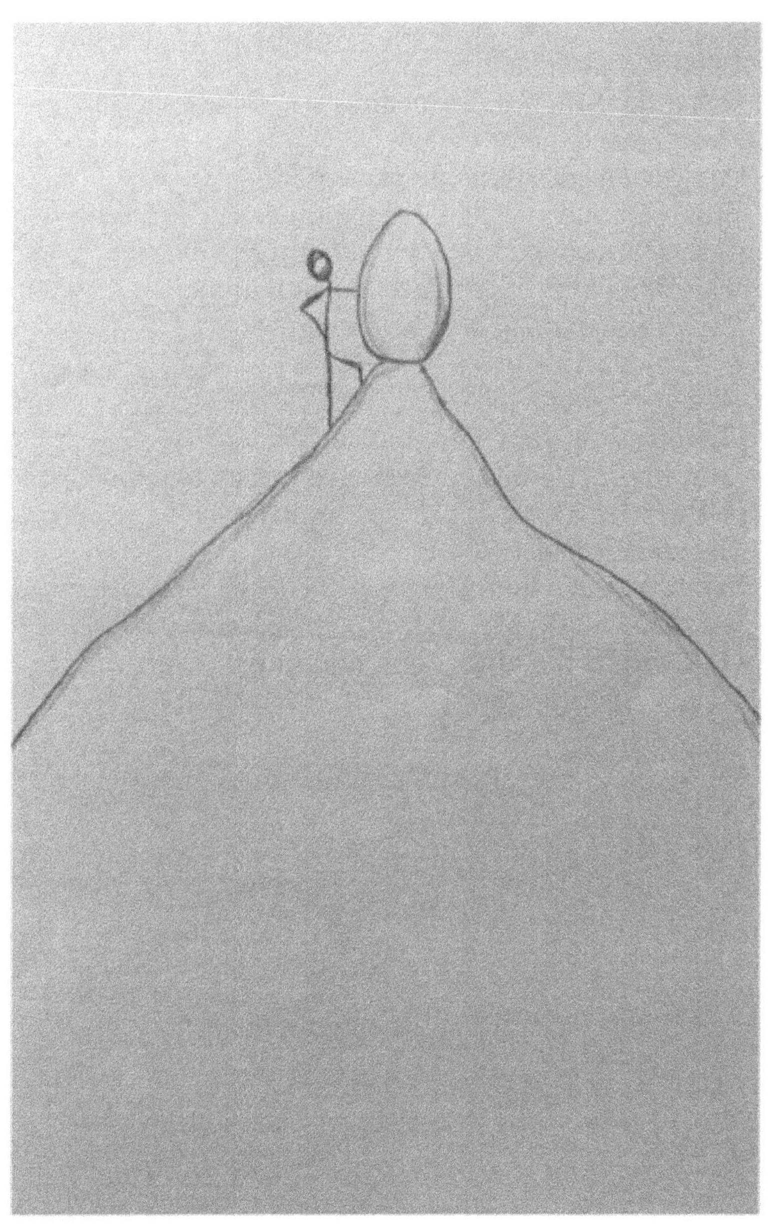

On This Day - 14/03/14 - I Thought:

"You have to play the game."
What does that really mean?
"You have to go to the parties
And make sure that you're seen."
How can one ever achieve happiness
If they are constantly trying to impress?
Thankfully my experience has taught me
That this needs to be addressed.

For me to get a job
Involves an element of begging.
But I refuse to let that spill over to my real life
Otherwise Destination: Constantly Needing Approval
Is where I'll be heading.
Therefore it's important that I continue to love myself
And always do MY best.
Looking in the mirror and nodding in approval
Is my favourite kind of test.

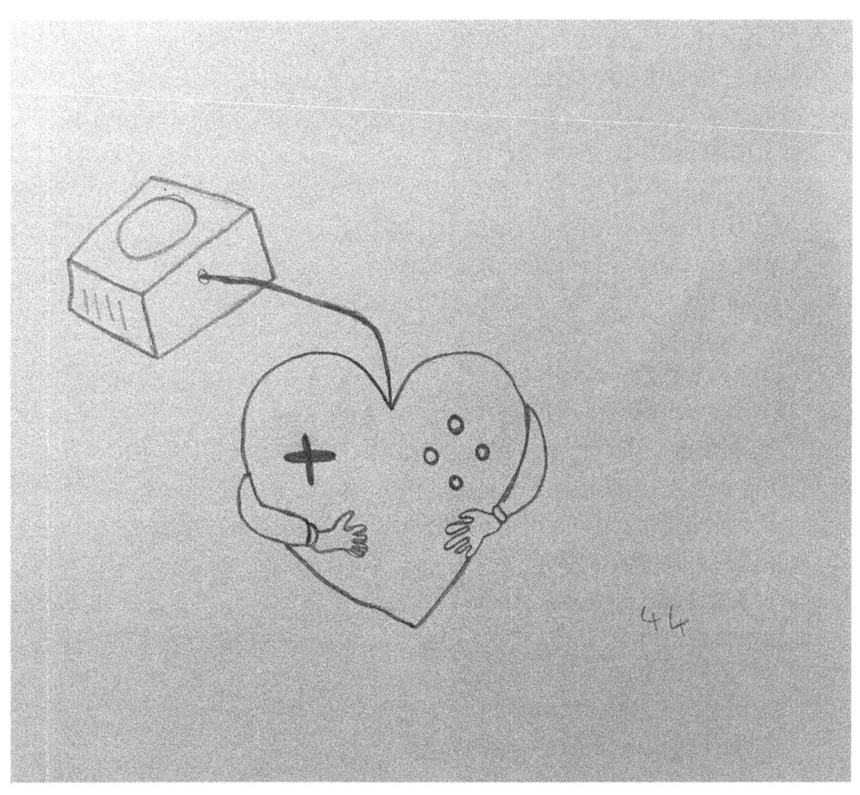
44

On This Day - 14/03/14 - I Thought:

This world is full of judgement,
But based on whose rule?

"Only God can judge me."

I don't say that's wrong or right
But having a clear conscience
Is what helps me sleep at night.

The fact is nobody can definitively come to a conclusion
About whether a Higher Power exists.
Truth be told this is less and less of concern to me
But what bothers *I* is this:
When it comes to conforming to societies values
Many cannot resist.
"It's great to be an individual,"
Is what to my face they insist.
We all nod in agreement
But when time comes for action
Most people seem to desist.
Make your own decisions, I say,
Don't follow the crowd.
I stick to my guns,
I am my own man
And this makes me proud.

I accept judgement from nobody
My conscience is my only arbiter.
I have faith in my mind
Because it follows me everywhere
Therefore it's my sole babysitter.

On This Day - 28/04/14 - I Thought:

The less you expect from people
The less likely you are to be let down.
Thinking in this somewhat negative way
Makes me feel like the loneliest person in town,
Therefore deep in this sea of regret I drown.

But late at night, whilst laying on my back
I reconcile myself to this sad fact.
Ultimately I search for the strength within,
I don't rely on others for me to win.
In the mirror I look at him:

Yes fact.

I confirm that this lone soldier stance is not an act.

On This Day - 28/04/14 - I Thought:

I'm finding it more and more difficult
To think big over here.
I've long since hit the Glass Ceiling I fear.
I remember the days when I felt indestructible
But this place has a way of bursting your bubble.

One is not allowed to talk themselves up
Or demonstrate self love.
You must remain detained at the station
And never get above.
You must be self deprecating
To show that you you are humble.
Never, ever, celebrate your success
Or "arrogant" they will mumble.

I have now come to the conclusion
That we are not catered for or particularly desired.
And to all those keeping up false pretences
I am sick and tired.
Faces that do not resemble mine
Leave me uninspired.
But it's difficult to talk to those who may relate
Because we are all so desperate to get hired.

It makes me sick,

I hate this shit

But what gets me out of bed is
Remembering that my life has been a hit.
Over here ambition may not match mine
But I. do. not. accept. it.

On This Day - 04/06/14 - I Thought:

Recently I've been contemplating
Something I never thought I'd do:

I'm wondering if I've had it easy hitherto.

Making a conscious effort to step out of the isolation,
Has given a different voice to what I question.
I've been cocooned in my head,
Within my thoughts only I reside -
"Hey, where have you been?"
But it was never my intention to hide.
And come to think of it,
It's not that bad outside.

I'm not the only one who hustles,
There are others working hard.
It's all been clouded by the fact that I'm scarred.

I have to believe that once again I'll rise,
Because there is no happiness in dwelling on the fall.
That's why I now look at my contemporaries
And say, "I respect them all."

Despite me believing that at this juncture
It's much healthier to take up this position,
It doesn't mean that I have to be submissive.

Bring on the competition!

On This Day - 18/07/14 - I Thought:

My fathers funeral cost four thousand pounds,
I know this because I paid for it.
I was only sixteen years old at the time
But I was left to take care of it.

That was eleven years ago,
And I'm incredibly proud of the way
I've continued to grow.

Could I have gone further if my father was still here?
I guess I'll never know.

Appreciation from the blood that remains?

I'm going to have to say “no."

Support from friends
As I've navigated adulthood thus far?

I can't say I can distinguish a pal from a foe.

Leaning more towards the belief again I'll rise
Is a thought that keeps me alive.
Age fourteen: stabbed
Fifteen: expelled
Sixteen: dad dead -
I've always had to survive.
Although I believe in my strength
More than anything else,
I'm balanced because 'Bonnie's' been by my side.

I'll always look for the good in people
Because it's a happier way to be.
But when it comes to looking for support
I'll never look beyond Bonnie and me.

On This Day - 18/07/14 - I Thought:

Along the ocean of uncertainty
I continue to set sail.
As I float along the rocky sea I ask myself:

"Does everyone want me to fail?"

But truth be told even if they did

It wouldn't be my problem

Because normally when one wishes somebody else bad
The problem usually lies with them.

It is also important for me to consider
How unhelpful it can be,
To contemplate such negativity.

So as I drift amongst the waves
I now have to ask:
"Does the problem lie with me?"

I think I spend ninety percent of time on my lonesome.
The good thing about this is that I form my own opinion.

It's so quiet that it's loud

For the most part my existence is solitary,
At the start this was chosen by me.
Therefore I can truly say that this is my identity.

On This day - 21/10/14 - I Thought:

My morals prevented me
From complaining behind their back,
I'm not sure I could ever bury my honesty
Just to move in a pack.

But with every pro theres a con,
And the fact that I'm now a recluse is one.
I dwell on this as the silence goes on:
Is this present emptiness,
Or constant empty conversations more fun?

You would need a torch to read my mind

Because it's as dark and lonely as the night.

You'll also find me repeatedly asking myself:

If there's nobody around to judge my opinions,

Who's wrong and who's right?

At this moment in time I concede defeat to balance,

And I'll go on to say that my single-mindedness

Is a poisoned chalice.

On This Day - 21/10/14 - I Thought:

Crucial to my job is "staying in the moment."
But when this job is a career

There is something one cannot escape,

There is this constant fear.

How long will this last?
Is this job my last?
How can he have a bigger role than me
When you consider what I've done in the past?

These questions are not unique
When one's job is to act,
So then
How can "staying in the moment" ever be a fact?

I've always planned for the future,
But I used to enjoy the present more -
This is a result of my past
Causing my paranoia to go through the floor.

All I've ever tried to do is be smart,

Hand on my heart.

And I truly believe this sets me apart.
But I think I may have detoured if I knew
What I know now
At the start.

"Moment to moment"
And planning for the inevitable dry spells
Constantly duel for me.

In the midst of this never-ending battle
I'm losing myself,

Which is why every single day

I seriously consider doing something else.

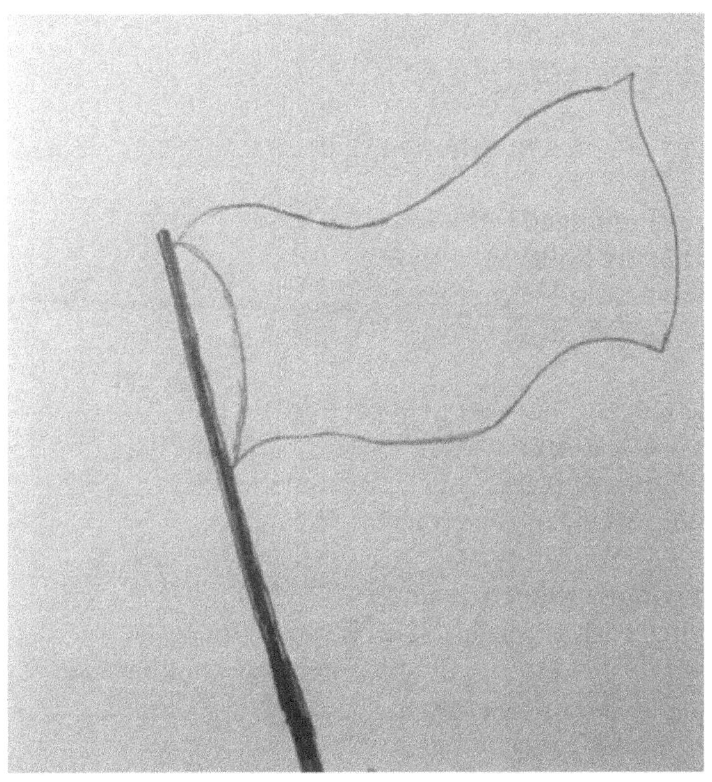

On This Day - 21/10/14 - I Thought:

"Keep going, you'll make it!"
(It seems that they faked it)
"Oh my, a star is born!"
(This is a quote I now mourn)

When you are a kid with potential
Everybody roots for you.
When you convert that potential -

Root for you? They used to.

This made me question myself:

Have I changed?
Is this my fault?
What would I rather have;
A large following or a cult?

The fact is I couldn't be a prodigy forever,
I've evolved into a man.
And it's completely out of my hands
Whether or not that costs me a fan.

Growing without guidance
Comes with a myriad of difficulties,
Everyday I fight to navigate myself through these.
This needs my attention,
Not others' insecurities.

There have been a handful of mentor candidates -
And I'll always keep an open mind.
But those relationships expired the same way.
So it's no wonder
I now keep those type of people at bay.

On This Day - 21/10/14 - I Thought:

Banter, companionship, hedonism, growing pains,
Young fun.
Part of the circle showed no loyalty

So it's done.

Just when it seemed I had the boxes
Work and Play ticked
It all got ruined by this dumb and disloyal prick.

Now the easiest piece of advice to give is to
"Just get over it."
But how about if every time you see that person
You want to be sick?
Consider if that individual
Is a large reason you're paranoid...

What do you suggest - confront or avoid?

I am expressive and sensitive

And this is my diary.

So if you've read up to here

You may now decide you've had enough of me.

But I cannot let my friends down.
I could never live with myself.
And if I did disappoint them
I really hope I wouldn't blame anyone else.

I wonder who am I to think others should live by my code.
This is why the majority of my days are on silent mode.

It's draining to be over analytical
And question all my relationships.
This is why me connecting with people
Is as rare as flying in a spaceship.

I am still a young man
So there is definitely time.
This prick would probably be surprised to know
That he stole a part of youth.

But it's okay, I'm taking it back because it's mine.

On This Day - 21/10/14 - I Thought:

This was an example of a reunion feeling like a vacuum,
We never went to the same school
But it was like being back in a classroom.

"Did you know such and such earns this much?"

"That one drives a Range."

"That one flies a plane"

"And that one has changed."

A group of males now in their late twenties,
Gossiping and reminiscing
About what they did when they were ten.
Can count on one hand
How many reunions there have been since then.

"Bro!"

"My boy!"

"I love you!"

But if this is so
How come
Every single thing I'm telling you about my life
You did not know?
Why is it that you all ask what fame is like
But not once have ever called and asked

"How's your health, Mike?"

"Yeah man, back in the day..." (they hang on to the past)

But when I open up you have nothing to say.

We don't relate career-wise
We don't relate emotion wise.

In fact, our relationships have expired,
Lets part ways.

Isn't that wise?

On This Day - 13/11/2014 - I Thought:

We both bonded over hopes and dreams
"We're going to make it to the top."
But you kept your eyes trained on me,
You admired me so,

It got too much - I wanted it to stop.

I actually never felt the same about you
But we had an ambition in common.
The main problem is that when you wanted inspiration

It was me you would always summon.

It's a compliment I know
But what about me?

Come on!

I was and am younger than you,
So I needed inspiration too.
It made me feel nauseous that whatever you did
Was based on what I would do too.

Things snowballed for me
And although I don't blame you,
I didn't like your expression.
Therefore I retreated from you
And anybody else similar

I became uncomfortable
With the stares and comparisons.

For a while there has been fame and money at stake
And I'm a loner so maybe it's my mistake
But I've isolated myself

Because I can't stand and don't want to be fake.

Beyond these words

You've been on my mind throughout
And I think things are going well for you
While I struggle with self doubt.
It hurts, it stinks, it makes me sick
But competing with my friends
Is something I can do without.

On This Day - 13/11/2014 - I Thought:

I have come to terms with the fact
That I'm not a team player.
I'd rather go it alone

And be the dragon slayer.

But this comes with problems

Because if you peel off my top layer

My turmoil is revealed

And perhaps I have not a hope or a prayer.

In my life loneliness has long been a recurring theme

And that's because the opposite of this

Requires an element of being a team.

Relationship - team
Family - team
Friendship - team

And although I know why,

Almost all of the above are absent from my life

So I think it is actually my dream to embrace a team

Otherwise the one on the list that I can actually tick

Will finally fall off its' balance beam.

On This Day - 17/06/15 - I Thought:

"I am the only one who makes my life interesting,"

Is a warped thought that I've long believed

But I now need to consider other ideas

Because this bandage is starting to bleed.
It's a plaster that I've covered the cracks with,
My strength has started to recede

I'm now thinking there is more to life than:
"Everyday you have got to achieve."

On what basis does one reach that target?
Even then I'll move the goal-posts I bet.

Married,
Healthy,
Well-under thirty,

Amongst the carnival of thoughts I forget.

If I'm the only one that brings joy to my life,
What is the point of having a wife?
What's the point of talking to anyone if
Absolutely nobody else brings me any fun?

So that theory can't be true
Because I'm sitting here alone with a loose screw.
Now I've tucked that thought in,

I'm not the sole one
Who brings me fun.

Now...how about inspiration?

On This Day - 23/06/15 - I Thought:

"Hey aren't you that guy..?
Wait, don't tell me... I know you're on tv,"
Is what I get often
Or sporadically.
Although it's soothing to my ego,
If I'm not working
I'd rather somebody would just leave me be.
Caught between two worlds:
Fame and reality.
But climbing Everest to get the job
Is pretty much always what happens in actuality.
I'm not attempting deception,
I'm just addressing the perception,
Trust me,
I don't believe in self-deprecation,
I'm simply bringing to attention
The fact that a career like mine
Can leave your life in suspension.
This is why when I'm around people outside my game
I'm filled with apprehension.
But in my game many people act the same
So if one doesn't
"You are not playing the game."
So if I don't fit in that world,
And I don't fit in this world
What chance do I have of staying sane?
A handful of times I've taken comfort in the fact
That a certain confidant sees where I'm coming from.
But then despite constant monologues of communication
"I could never feel that way about my mum."
One minute they understand,
Get excited and hyped up -
At least to your face
But then they call you arrogant, aggressive,
As soon as you leave the place.

They know deep down they are comparing and competing -
"We're saving for a mortgage...
I'm not ready to get married...Your Porsche cost how much?"
These questions asked for no apparent reason.
I try my best to dilute,
I've dumbed down for certain individuals
But there's not much you can do
If somebody constantly brings up your residuals.
Then I have to put them in their place.
But then I feel bad.
But I have to remind them that
Despite their claims of individualism
And self sustenance
They are getting help from their dad.
Long before any fallout I always planned to step back,
Especially when they talk about their
So-called-friends behind their back.
At this juncture I think the best thing to do
Is accept that I'm a one man crew.
No more schooling others. Who is schooling me?
Despite all that, look: I, MYSELF,
Have actually made money.
I really have to stick to my level,
Let boys figure themselves out.
Because their nonsensical behaviour is driven by self-doubt.
So when it comes to friends, on my hand I count one.
And if an organic and genuine kinship is going to come
It will come.

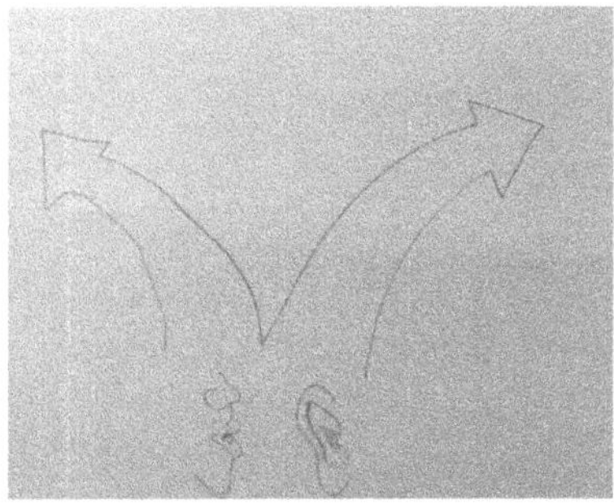

On This Day - 22/07/15 - I Thought:

The majority of my life is shrouded in solitude,
In these dark times I try to focus on fortitude.
But when the only sound in the room
Is the hand of the clock,
And the sound of your heart ,
It's hard to change your mood.

This truth is always waiting in the wings,
I'm running out of words to describe the pain that brings,
And that is why I hang on tightly to these two things:

1) Since I'm mostly alone
I can guarantee that my opinions are my own.

And

2) Since alone is how my time is mostly spent
There is nobody that can negatively influence.

It's not lost on me how this can read pitiful,

So allow me as I wait for a miracle

To champion the fact that I'm an individual.

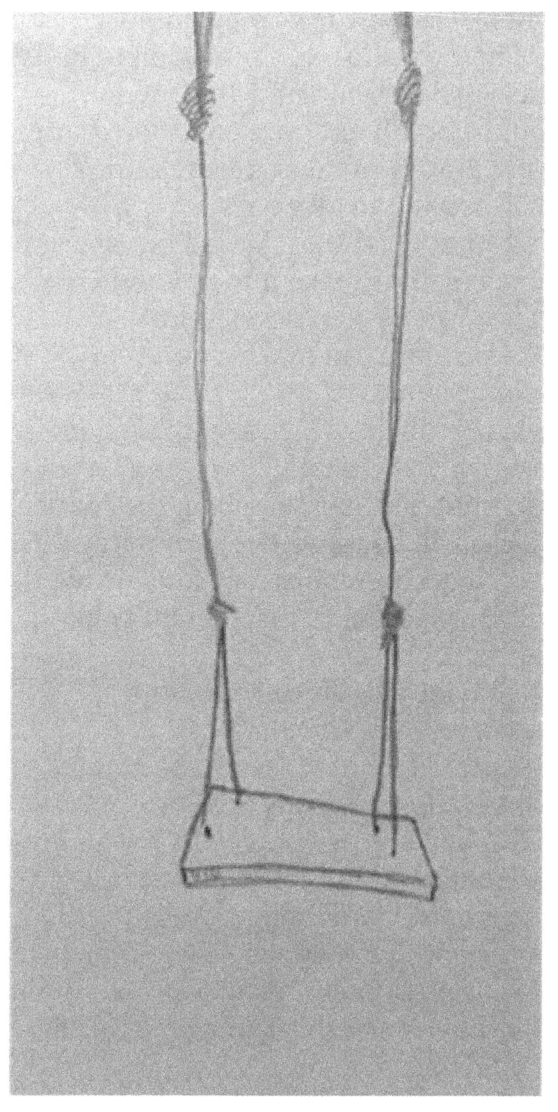

On This Day - 03/06/15 - I Thought:

If you're black and you're recognised
There is one question you're certain to be asked -
"Do you consider yourself a role model?"
The enquirers will not once consider your past.
It will not matter to them if fame came slow or fast.
They will ask you to give back
Whether or not you were kicked out of class.
Not one person will take into account
That it is a twenty-four seven effort
To make sure you can make a payment
Into your account.
That when you're black and on television
You inevitably stand out,
Because right now lets switch on the channels
And blacks will be represented by a tiny amount.
Once you have been on screen and graced the stage,
You will be expected to inspire and behave,
And especially because
I've been doing this since I was nine,
It's messed up their calculations,
So I'm expected to meet their expectations -
It doesn't matter about my age.
Even if I've had to learn how to be a man myself,
I will be labelled "ungrateful" and a "sell-out",
Unless I give the youth help.
Whether or not I've been out of work for a while,
I'm a black actor and writer so I have to smile.
No matter how much this game may cause
One's confidence to dent,
If you are a celebrity kid's look up to you,
So their mum's and dad's want you to be an extra parent.
Before being anything I am a human being,
And just like you I'm a product of where I've been.
When they watch you on the tv screen,

It's like they're seeing a robot,
A machine.
The adulation can be amazing,
A huge boost to my ego.
But getting recognised will never make my demons go.
It won't bring my father back,
It won't get my family on track.

I'm a person just like you,

I'm afraid of death just like you.

But unlike you my mistakes could be broadcast,
In this digital age I could be humiliated fast.

I need inspiration too,
I need a hero too.

Consider this when cursing through the screen at
The athlete or artist you look up to.

On This Day - 12/09/15 - I Thought:

My love/hate relationship is with luck.
So when I want a bad run to change I'm stuck.
If ever I'm experiencing a rut,
I very much struggle to hope for good luck.
It's difficult for me to be convinced of other than what I believe -
It's not luck
But an accumulation of hard work
That leads you to achieve.

My temperature rises when I'm told to cool down
And that "sometimes things just happen."
If that's the case let's all give up any chase
Because that theory means that
Everything will find its rightful place.
But then I'm told that "God loves a trier."
So now forget my temperature rising,

I'm on fire.

Because it seems to me that any advice giver is a liar.
Now I don't ask for advice
I don't see the point.
I must admit I do feel guilty
For knocking a mantra chanter's chi out of joint.
Then reconcile it by chanting that if one really believes
They really don't need another person to validate their point.
Okay. I know I don't believe in luck,

Then why discuss it?

Because deep down I want somebody to prove me wrong:
Make me take my own belief and stuff it.

Make me change my mind,

Get in my boat and rock it.

I think you make your own luck -
But how can I make something that I do not believe exists?
Am I too young to think in a bitter way such as this?
I'm not trying to convert anybody's thinking,
But when I conform my questions persist.
Look,
The truth is this:

I've had to work for every single victory,

And overall that's fine by me.
But at times I look at other people's current position,
And simply wonder if I've been unlucky.
But if I don't believe in good luck,

Can there be bad luck?

You may not think it's such a big deal,

But can you at least see why I'm stuck?

On This Day - 15/10/15 - I Thought:

"We Brits are very tolerant."
But what is it you're tolerating?
Before I'm accused of playing a card,
I want you to think long and hard -
If you say that you are tolerant to the likes of me
That means you're suggesting I've done something bad.
Let's be honest and not veer off track,
If you're tolerant of me you're implying
It's bad to be black.
Now you may pull out your dictionary,
And immediately challenge me.
You flip pages and point to the meaning,
"This definition proves I'm not being demeaning:"

TOLERANCE
noun

1. the ability or willingness to tolerate the existence of opinions or behaviour that one dislikes or disagrees with.

2. the capacity to endure continued subjection to something such as a drug or environmental conditions without adverse reaction.

So you tolerate me because you dislike me?
Disagree with me?
My skin being different from yours is akin
To you having to endure drugs?
My features are changing your environment?
I was born in Camden,
That makes me British
But my fellow Brit can't distinguish
Between me and liquorice
But fortunately for me I've grown my skin to the point
Where it's too thick for my self worth to diminish.

When I walk on by and am looked upon with distaste,
When I'm minding my own business
But can sense the hate.
I look for a mirror and talk to my best mate:
"Michael, be calm, tolerate."
I plan on sticking around -
I've always been known to persist.
But my knowledge of their so-called tolerance
Makes it a battle to exist.
I'm learning more and more that life is a marathon,
And I'm planning to last the distance.

Aren't *I* the one who is practising tolerance?

On This Day - 21/10/15 - I Thought:

I stick to them because my morals are high
But if I'm the only one who agrees
Then it's not enough to get by.
I struggle to forgive,
And although I wish I didn't
I no longer question why.

As children we were so sensitive,
And of course that's no crime.
But often after a fallout
We wouldn't speak for months at a time.
A child learns from their parent(s) -

That's the bottom line.

My father was estranged from all his relatives,
So his children ignoring each other seemed fine.

We all had our own cups -
I honestly thought this was normal
Until the person that taught me about family
Told me this was more than formal.
Now when I think back,
From the beginning of my time

Our parents didn't put a stop to the notion:

"What's yours is yours
And what's mine is mine."

As I enter my next phase
And teach myself to become a man,
I'm so fearful of my pathetic blueprint
That I constantly try to come up with a plan:

I will talk to my children,
They will talk to each other.
These are tactics that my adults did not employ.

So with all this in mind,

I will

Because I am not going to mess up my little girl or boy.

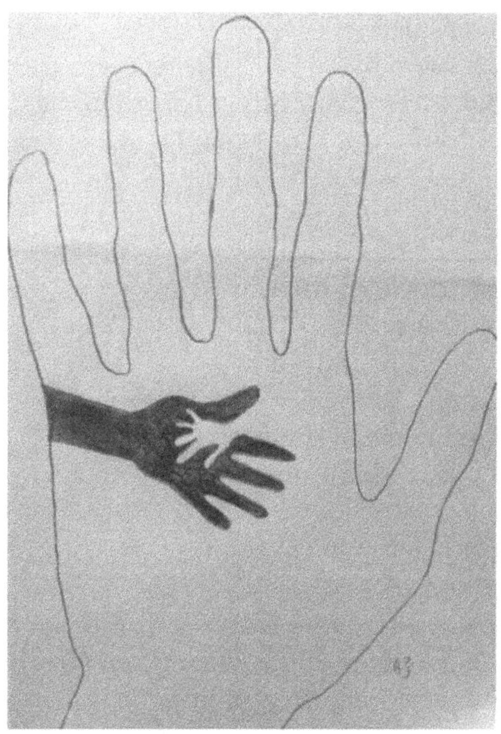

On This Day - 19/11/15 - I Thought:

A Letter From The Other Side

Dear Son,

I always knew you would be special,
From an infant you were an intelligent rebel.
Forever asking questions,
Why? Why? Why?
You were always determined
Not to let learning pass you by.
I knew you would look after the family if I were to die,
On June 26th 2003 I found out that wasn't a lie.
I remember when I used to take you to your
Thursday classes,
On the the Northern Line to Edgware.
The day I had a heart attack on the way
I wasn't sure we'd get there.
After the fourth audition I collapsed -
Another bout of angina.
The newsreader helped you call the ambulance
Because you were a 9 year old minor.
So on that day
We both learned that the attacks on the way,
Were just a way to prepare.
So in hindsight all the arrests were worth it in Edgware.
I could see that you were becoming stronger and stronger.
Observant I was of your dedication and hunger.
But I was a scholar -
Highly educated, My fathers' son. Now young man,
I want you to be one.

The time away from your school to film had me torn,
But you were starting to earn and support.
Perhaps this is why you were born.

Like me you were a fighter, Never a victim,
Never back down.
But your intelligence, popularity, talent, and charisma
Caused revulsion And led to your expulsion.
My heart erupted again, A volcanic explosion.
You went on to do your plays, I saw them live.
In fact Fallout was the last time you played
When I was alive.
But I've been watching you from up here,
Supporting "Baby" and your siblings.
Avoiding trouble, falling in love, getting married.
I've watched you be lonely - Just like I was.
Yes my young son, I've observed all this from above.
I can safely say, That you'll keep making your way.
Even when your world is dark I watch you light a path
Through each day.
I genuinely love you, And I always will. I'm very sorry
That I didn't leave a will.
I know how much you value unconditional love.
I loved you and will continue to do so from the other side,
Through good times and bad.
I'm incredibly proud of you,

Your Dad.

This is an imaginary letter I've received from my father.
If I were to receive a message from him
A positive one like this is what I'd rather.
But honestly,
Although this may change - I don't currently ponder
What he may think of me from wherever he is.
Maybe this is a way of me trying to get on with my biz.Maybe it's because I don't really believe in the afterlife. Or maybe it's because I'm too busy chasing life.

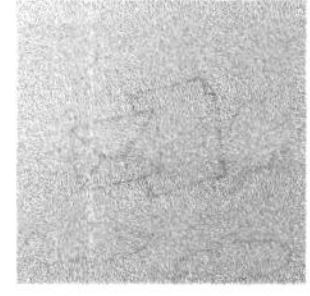

On This Day - 20/11/15 - I Thought:

When I'm walking back from the station at night,
I'll no longer cross the road to avoid causing a fright.
When I speak I'll sound like myself,
If the audio is "too street"
That's a problem for someone else.
I will continue to communicate
In my slightly low and confident Voice,
And if I want to use slang
That's simply my choice.

Life is complicated enough
Without the addition of egg shells,
And just because I'm black it doesn't mean I have
A quota of "fucking hells!"
If I'm angry it's up to me to deal with it like an adult,

But if I'm labelled an "Angry Black Man"
That isn't and has never been my fault.

Nobody chose their colour
But I wear mine with pride.
Whenever I'm in the door I'll continue to never hide.

I spent so long running away from stereotypes,
But I was so glad to learn that my face was never
MY gripe.
I cracked the code,
Lightened the load,
Now I can take flight.

Each and everyone of us
Is just trying to figure all this out,

Each and everyone of us has an element of self-doubt.

So basically we'd all likely agree that understanding
Our existence is hard -

Therefore do not have the audacity to think you have
A right to accuse anybody like me of "playing a card."

I really hope and pray
That we'll have children one day.
And to those little black treasures I definitely say:
Others will try to make your shade a burden,

But don't. ever. let them have their way.

On This Day - 28/12/15 - I Thought:

A cknowledge that I'm always trying my
B est. Be less hard on myself and afford myself rest.
C onsider the fact that I'm passing if life is a test.
D efinitely understand that idiot was the last. That "individual' and
E veryone similar must be consigned to the past.
F amily is more than just a word. Flip lip service payers the bird.
G rowth is not what I'm aiming for it's what I'm constantly going through.
H olistic living is from the endoscopy not something "cool" to do.
I ntelligence is what I have, we all know what we think we posses.
J ealousy is a natural emotion but not dealing with it will leave you a mess.
K illing me is what I feel is happening when I've experienced this from almost
every single person I've known.
L osing so-called friends due to that is necessary because a liar is what I cannot
condone.
M illion pounds by twenty six that's where that subject ends. Rueful chuckle is
what I'm doing: "I'm rich, no wonder I have no friends."
N ever mind what others are doing unless you like insanity.
O pen Box Productions is where you'll hear more thoughts from me.
P lease look in the mirror and always tell the truth.
Q uestion your behaviour if social media is your truth.
R esist the temptation to be upset if
S omeone loves their self.
T o be honest I think you need help if you want people to dislike their self.

U ltimately work on yourself and stop trying to find fault with others.
V ultures is a gear change that I want to make:
they swoop
W hen you're flying but never help you in trying. Watch out for them the same way
you would a snake.
X anex is what I feel I've taken when couch potatoes try to give advice.
Y ou know if you're qualified, so piss off if you're not, don't make me ask twice.
As a black man I'm interested in my own history - my identity they will never
taketh. I'm looking at my reflection: currently I'm at my
Z enith.

On This Day - 23/02/16 - I Thought:

What is a “real” friendship? I’ve always dared to ask.
Experiencing an authentic kinship
Often feels like an impossible task.
It seems to me a lot of people want to avoid this question
Because breaking it down will call every single
One of your relationships into Question.
Cyberspace has blurred the lines
And nobody wants to be lonely.
Scrolling through screens, seeing smiling faces:
“What about me?”
The person enquiring had six hundred “friends”
And counting
And they still asked “what about me?”
So I’ve been wondering whether friendship
Is just a word and what people want Others to see:
Hashtag Squad Goals. Hashtag Power Couple.
Capture the “busy” side of the room.
Sometimes these pictures are shared,
And behind closed doors
The Tour Guide tells you who they like and “hate”
I was always left uncomfortable
Because the image was from a recent date.
The above two-facedness affects me too much
Because the pursuit of a real interaction
Has left me with enough on my plate.
Therefore I retreat
No more schooling
I simply cannot relate.
And then I’m fucked because I can’t forgive
And I mostly don’t want to in this context.
But then I’m lonely
Just like the person who scrolled
Through screens and asked “What about me?”

So now I ask - "what about me?"
Well - I've never been interested in capturing
The "busy" side of the room.
I made her my wife
She made me her groom.
Hashtag Power couple?
Nah, it'll be thirteen years soon :)
She's been the same when I'm rich
The same when I'm poor
We accept each others flaws.

So, what is a true friendship?

Based on what I've seen and heard fuck all that,

I'm married to my lover and my only true friend -

How many people can claim that as a fact?

On This Day - 6/10/16 - I Thought:

In two days I will be kissing you goodbye,
I won't miss you I cannot lie.
I know that is easy to say when you're still young
But wow - to have survived my twenties
I think I was strong
I couldn't relate to the struggle in the same way
Because very early I was working for good pay.
I spoke about tax when they were talking about uni,
I was getting unusual attention and trying not to go loony.
They worried about jobs
I worried about what people wanted from me.
I saw the face expressions when I bought my first house
"Michael I know you're going to make it!"
When I resembled something similar
They were as quiet as a mouse.
All the social media stuff never sat right with me
I was signing contracts and paying mortgages
While they were wondering
How they were supposed to be
I had fully grown adults asking me for advice
I was making and taking opportunities
Because I taught myself to roll the dice
I was and am an old soul so nobody gave *ME* advice
Gossip
"Yolo"
Immature verbal right hooks
"Michael, oh my God, which twenty-two year old
Writes books?"
But when we fell out,
"Michael, you think you're clever because you write
And read books!"
Our youth wanted attention
But my job brought me attention.

No. I got attention already
But I started at nine so before acting who was me?
“The thirties are the best years of your life
‘Cos you’ve sorted all your shit!”
But I’m sure there will be more shit.
I never properly mourned my loss
So I think others forgot
“You’re rich and famous, what problems have you got?!”
I got married at twenty-seven
My “friends” questioned themselves.
I got recognised when we were together
My “friends” questioned themselves.
The best thing about being older
Is that it’s easier to understand that a lot
Of the criticisms were about themselves.
I’ve been confused in my twenties,
I’m still confused now.
But I feel strong and beautiful,
It’s easy to say because I’m young and I’m beautiful.
But in two days time will I miss my twenties?
No way!
No how!

p.s.

ask me again in my forties :)

On This Day - 21/12/16 - I Thought:

I wish I were a crier
Instead of always feeling the need to fight
Because if this was the case
Then I'd possibly sleep at night
In my real life I struggle to adjust my personality -

Ultimately I really do love me

But if this is really true

Then why am I so lonely?

Now comes the self-judgement:

"Do I not appreciate what I've got?"

Yes I do

That's why I guard it jealously
The problem is this makes me feel like a robot
I take pleasure in the fact that I get to be other people
And step out of my actual life's rigidity
I feel it's unhealthy
But if it wasn't for this discipline
Who the fuck would have saved me?

I wish I were a crier
Instead of always feeling the need to fight
Because if this was the case
I'd be dreaming right now
And not ruminating all night

On This Day - 19/01/17 - I Thought:

Often staring into space lost in thought after thought
Looking for someone to blame
For my perceived lack of support
I've been searching for that friend and/or connection
But it's so hard to organically find
Sometimes I realise I've been in the same spot for hours
While life leaves me behind

I was recently told I expect too much
When we were debating loyalty
My stomach turned
Those words burned

But who is happier - them or me?

I mention what makes me uneasy
And that in turn makes them uneasy
This happens more than nine out of ten times for me
I'm an outlier much more easily

Far more often than I'm comfortable with

The days are the same: fast forward or rewind

It's me asking myself:
"Why is that true friend so hard to find?"

But right this second something has occurred to me -

Perhaps a true friend is only in my mind

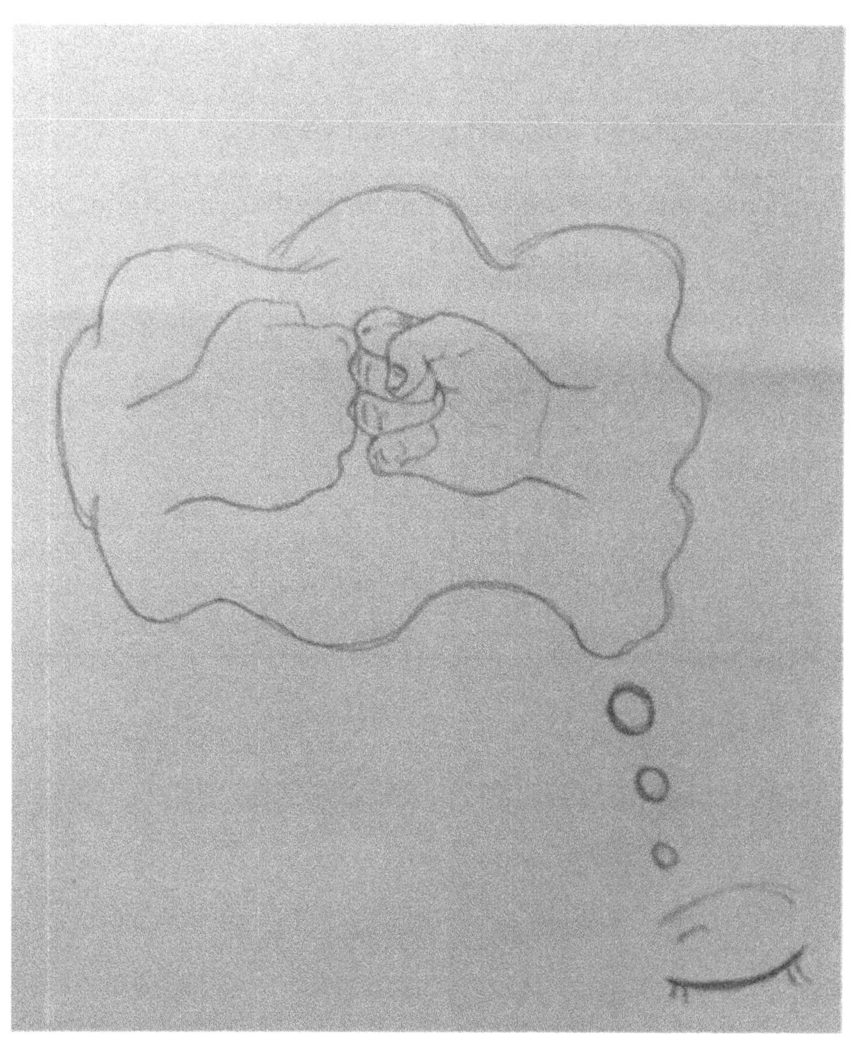

On This Day - 19/04/17 - I Thought:

I think I'm the smartest person I've met
With no formal education.
I enter any room and feel this without any hesitation.

Then my depression is confirmed
Because I seem to be the only one concerned.

"These people don't understand?!"

By that logic they're clueless

"Yes, and it means that I'm the best
Because I got this far without passing a test."

So what?

Well...

This loneliness is hell.

So

Nothing.

Really if I'm that smart,

If I am so elevated from the rest,

So far apart,

Why have I not found a way
To rejuvenate my rotten heart?

Why have I refuted all playing of The Game?

Why didn't I just do it and give it another name?
Why haven't I worked out a way to exist as comfortably
As possible within my Paradigm?

Maybe all this time I thought I was so smart

I was actually getting left behind.

On This Day - 15/05/17 - I Thought:

I wish I could operate on my pain.
I wish I could remove it, bury it
And look down on it like disdain.

But if from that emotion I were to refrain
How would I distinguish pleasure from pain?
So how about putting it six feet under ground
And visiting it every so often?
But by that logic I should visit my father's grave.
But I don't.
We don't.
We don't talk about it.

So how about acceptance?

But I don't think it's acceptable.

Does that make me bitter?

Or is it that I'm not a quitter?
Has acceptance got anything to do with quitting?

I don't particularly like thinking too much anymore

This headache is splitting.

A cerebral war takes place in my head

Even though it looks like I'm just sitting

Deep down I think I'm mostly right

But that's according to my eyesight

So for now I can put aside right or wrong

I'll accept this shit for now

But as for bitterness:

You better cut off my fucking tongue.

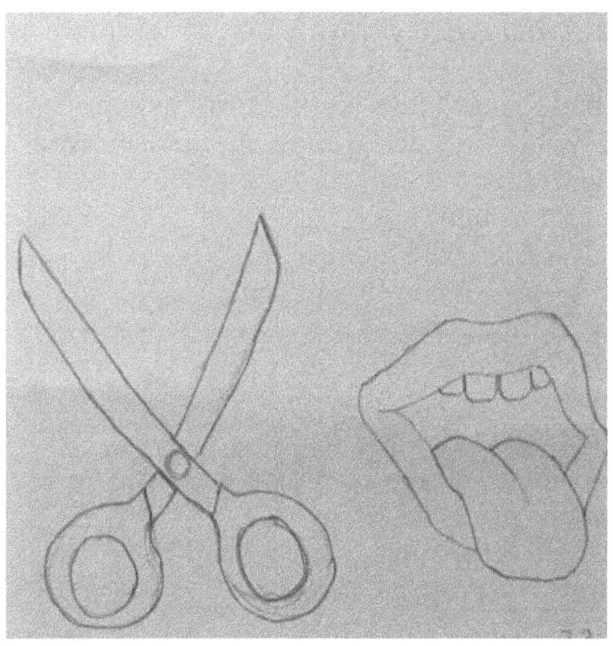

On This Day - 06/06/17 - I Thought:

I had a dream,
I was 9 years old and I was an actor.
Not long after I was an embryo
I was a literal thespian.
And while I was dreaming
"Literal" carried it's literal meaning
Within this dream some tried to turn it into a nightmare
But I was strong.
In this dream I had to teach myself right from wrong.
In this dream "My son is a star!" was my mother's tongue
During this trance
I never struggled for a chance
And to think it all started with a dance...
Soon this dream became a permanent state
It was incredibly thrilling
But I had to dodge the fakes
Fortunately I mostly knew how green my grass was
I just had to cut it to get rid of the snakes.
But this lawn mowing became a recurring theme...
In my reverie I was writing books
Walking down the street getting good and bad looks
I was called "funny"
And made lots of money
It's at this point of the dream when
Everybody started to get funny
There was a huge difference in my relationships
Before and after money
Throughout this dream I was treated like an adult
I was paying the mortgage age twelve
So it was okay for my carer's to default

In this dream school was a distraction -

It was hard to care about fractions

When before being a teen your job is "...and action!"
I woke up from all this at age twenty-six
That means the dream lasted seventeen years
And since then I've mainly been having to get through
The days
Realising my fears
Suddenly I found myself looking up to my peers
Sometimes I feel as if I took it all for granted
But mainly I know that's harsh
Because of how early I started
I hate the "realistic" life,
Just a house and a wife
Does this make me unappreciative?
Or is it inevitable because of my past life?
Now further confusion because I thought it was all a dream
So as I sit here and attempt to weep
My sanity I'm desperately trying to keep
I sadly reflect on how I often feel like a one one man team...
It's all so exhausting
I hope I can fall asleep again one day

So I can go back to my dream

On This Day - 12/01/18 - I Thought:

A new year so I naturally re-set.
Is it easier because I'll soon be back on set?
Unfortunately that pauses my upset.
Having my happiness hinge on this so much is a regret.

When I'm doing what I love I don't care about much else,
At those moments
I don't feel the need to refer to past wealth.
I don't question myself.
Or my mental health.

My shoulders aren't weighed down,

They feel light.

I seldom become more than irritated,

I hardly want to fight.

You see, it feels like I must keep working
So I can recognise myself.
I'm long fatigued by the precarity

I've tried to walk away
But away from this who is me?

For a long time I've realised I must find out
Because living like this for over two decades
Has been dangerous no doubt.

I've tried to demean it by tempering it's importance -

"Don't take it so seriously,"

But deep down that isn't me.

"Remain humble,"
"Stay down to earth."

All good but the unexplained periods of silence
Leads to the questioning of my self worth.

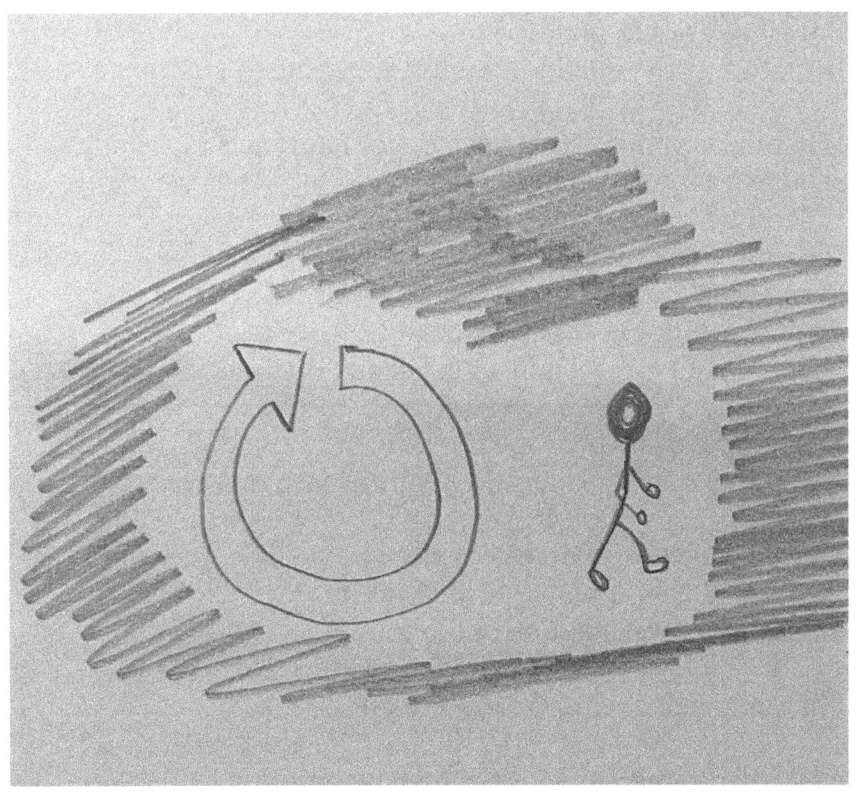

On This Day - 11/05/2020 - I Thought:

You came a few days early
Sensing my impatience
Recently I've been thinking
I haven't given myself enough credit for My patience!
I'm not so sure that's true
But what's not in doubt
Is that we truly, unconditionally, love you.

What I also think is that deep down I appreciate
All the "bad" as well as all the "good."
When I whispered this into your tiny ears
It seems you understood.
Everything that has happened has led me to this place,
To me enveloping you in my arms -
I can't imagine this smile ever leaving my face.

The other day I was asked,
"How do you feel bringing a baby girl into this scary world?"
I replied, "It feels great, how could I ever be scared or sad?
I have been chosen to be a dad."
"Who am I to complain? From now on
I'll always have sunshine in the rain."

I haven't slept a wink since she came -

And never more have I welcomed insomnia.

In fact maybe it's best I don't sleep
Because I may wake up to find it's all a dream
And my angel is not really here.
I've heard this changes everything
But truth be told
I felt the changes well over nine months ago.
I deserve no praise because I had to grow.

Throughout my life
Despite my blessings
About God I've often been second guessing.
But from now on I do not care about the name

Thank you to my wife and all the women who go through the pain.

I'm holding my daughter in my arms right this second
And never ever in my life have I felt spirituality or a
Higher Power so tangibly.

Once again, thank you so much.

I'll be forever grateful you chose me.

www.ingramcontent.com/pod-product-compliance
Lightning Source LLC
LaVergne TN
LVHW010702110826
845149LV00014B/3195

* 9 7 8 0 9 9 3 0 6 2 8 2 7 *